Not Exactly The CIA

A Revised History of Modern American Disasters

Roger Phelps

Not Exactly the CIA: A Revised History of Modern American Disasters
Copyright © 2019/2020 Roger Phelps. All Rights Reserved

Published by:
Trine Day LLC
PO Box 577
Walterville, OR 97489
1-800-556-2012
www.TrineDay.com
trineday@icloud.com

Library of Congress Control Number:2019952305

Phelps, Roger
 – 1st ed.
p. cm.
Includes references
Epub (ISBN-13) 978-1-63424-260-8
Mobi (ISBN-13) 978-1-63424-261-5
Print (ISBN-13) 978-1-63424-259-2
1. United States. -- Central Intelligence Agency -- History. 2. Intelligence service -- United States. 3. Politics and government 4. Psychological warfare -- United States -- History -- 21st century. 5. Political corruption -- United States. I. Phelps, Roger. II. Title

First Edition
10 9 8 7 6 5 4 3 2 1

Printed in the USA
Distribution to the Trade by:
Independent Publishers Group (IPG)
814 North Franklin Street
Chicago, Illinois 60610
312.337.0747
www.ipgbook.com

When sorrows come, they come not single spies
But in battalions.
                        – Hamlet, Act IV, Scene V

Contents

PREFACE

It seems to me that many social tensions today are the result of past coverups; occasions when persons with power to do so conceal under a superficial account the real nature of actions taken; much as an iceberg conceals its actual mass and danger under the surface of the ocean.

I came to write this book after assembling a chronology of events stretching between 1950 and 2016 involving efforts to increase US national security, such as well-known campaigns against communism and later, against terrorism. These were, of course, broadly based societal events, and so I was struck by the fact that the names of particular people occurred over and over for decades. I was struck, by how such a narrow slate of actors were responsible, seemingly, for broad social phenomena of American anti-communist and anti-terrorist agendas.

It seemed this narrow slate of actors deserved more focus. I read everything I could find. I decided I was seeing fragmented pieces of a not-reported whole.

Plato cautioned students to link things together only along natural, discoverable, and sufficiently evident joints (*Gr. arthroi*). I asked myself, can I legitimately join these pieces – actions involving the few actors I had noticed repeatedly – and say something about the whole they appear to form?

The record suggests that, for the purpose of scaring Americans into seeking security without questioning the circumstances, a clandestine act of domestic terrorism has been performed roughly every five years over the last four decades. It suggests that the perpetrators have been in positions where they could depend in various ways on agencies of national security. Such a group, the record suggests, includes former U.S. federal agents and their contacts – including foreign intelligence and military officials, both active and retired. In their public lives, these men advertise their patriotic anti-communism and counter-terrorism views.

Several good books have described some particular "path" to 9/11. This book describes one too, and it extends this scary path up to the present day, a time when in America truth has been dismissed in order that a Big Lie cannot be challenged.

The reader should know that official CIA covert operations made up comparatively little of the exploits and derring-do described in this book. With that said, the CIA and other intelligence agencies, some in foreign countries, made up a nurturing culture without which most of the exploits described could not have flourished, and in that way are inseparable from them. For the most part, the exploits were those of former intelligence operatives who were convinced national security policy was too weak. Time and again in my research, when facing a question of 'whodunit', it appeared with remarkable regularity and frequency that the entity most evidently having the power and the opportunity to have done it was this unofficial loose affiliation composed largely of former agents, which I have referred to in this book as "Not-Exactly-the-CIA."

The language in this book is mostly reportorial, journalistic; reporting facts, many of them attributed to persons who have specialized knowledge that an alleged fact is indeed a fact. But some recurring phrases are not purely journalistic, e.g., "It is likely that...." (borrowed from the field of law). And, in a very few cases, I have used a phrase like, "The following is speculation, but I believe it is well-founded" (borrowed from academic writing).[1]

With that said, I emphasize that this book does not rely on speculation. As such, it is my hope that the book will not be easily dismissed and that whatever small reputation it may acquire will be one fairly bestowed.

> *"To tell others that*
> *It is a rumor*
> *Will not do.*
> *When your own heart asks,*
> *How will you respond?"*[2]

---

1   I think it is fair to say this book's story is not easily or naturally deduced or introduced, and it might even be fair to say that the story is barely believable based on normal thinking. This of course defines "far-fetched" (Merriam-Webster Dictionary). But, so what – exactly?

2   From the *Hagakure* ("Hidden by the Leaves"), *Book of the Samurai*

Introduction

Blush not in actions darker than the night
Will shun no course to keep them from the light.
— Shakespeare, *Pericles*

Former FBI agent George Wackenhut, Cabazon Indian Security-Wackenhut Services Inc. joint venture

How Did We Get Here?

In 2016, before the close and controversial election of Donald Trump as U.S. president, nearly all Americans had asked themselves, "What happened to America?" Some meant "How did America lose jobs and global strength?" while others meant, "How did we lose democratic control of our government?"

To the second question, one answer starts in a seemingly unlikely place: the desert near the California-Mexico border, home of the poverty-stricken Cabazon Band of Mission Indians.

This reservation was exploited by political zealots, non-Indians, to further plans for America that were truly radical, but went largely unnoticed.

US Supreme Court Justice Louis Brandeis wrote, in 1928:

> The greatest dangers to liberty lurk in the insidious encroachment
> by men of zeal, well meaning, but without understanding.

Over the decades following World War II, exploits by history-makers Mao Zedong, Joseph McCarthy, Fidel Castro, Nikita Khrushchev, and John Kennedy inspired fervent zeal among U.S. anti-communists.

But the Vietnam war brought, among other horrors, news of the My Lai massacre and the murderous CIA Operation Phoenix. The public began to learn that through its "operations directorate," the CIA was doing much more than updating the president on how things stood in foreign countries – it was "doing something about" those countries. "Operations" were sacrosanct and secret, period; exempted from civilian oversight – even from CIA "analysis" agents. As former CIA agent Ray McGovern relates,

> I found it strange that subway-style turnstiles prevented analysts from going to the 'operations side of the house.'[1]

These let's-do-something-about-it agents often worked without direct supervision; in the words of then-CIA Director Bedell Smith, "the operational tail… wag(s) the intelligence dog."

Near-autonomous power for CIA's "operations" side, coupled with its extraordinary fear and hatred of any "soft-on-communism" policies, led to trouble.[2] Even after President Jimmy Carter forced out thousands of semi-rogue CIA operatives, neither their ambitions nor their power was ever curtailed.

Ops agent Theodore Shackley[3] warned after leaving the CIA in 1981,

> I am not alone. Since 1976 – and the election of President Jimmy Carter – approximately 2,800 career intelligence officers like myself have retired, many of them prematurely… Their experience … spanned decades. These men and women were professionals.[4]

Retaining agency contacts and abilities, the record shows, numerous fired operatives banded together and zealously continued anti-communist action. This power group was able to use their former agency and other government agencies as tools, as resource centers.

---

1   Ray McGovern, "The Deep State's JFK Triumph Over Trump," ConsortiumNews.com, October 30, 2017.

2   The news trickled out that Operation Phoenix murdered 20,587 civilians in Vietnam, by the admission of former CIA director William Colby, *New York Times* July 20, 1973. Viet Cong officials estimated between 40,000 and 60,000 civilians were killed or kidnapped under Operation Phoenix.

3   Born July 16, 1927, died December 9, 2002.

4   Theodore Shackley, *The Third Option*, self-published, 1981. That it required self-publishing indicates its stance was well out of the political mainstream – a radical stance. A front-leaf of one copy reads, "To Al (Haig), I hope this will keep you on the straight and narrow. Best of Luck, Ted Shackley, Washington DC, 9 September 1985."

Shackley boldly warned that ex-agents would use all resources available toward the following goal:

> Restoring a national policy that would project power into distant lands – restoring some control over events which threaten our very survival.[5]

Ted Shackley

Although, apparently, little attention was paid to this threat, effectively, it had the weight of the CIA behind it. For ensuing decades, the record shows both that the Shackleyesque crew fulfilled much of their threat and that even now, minus the deceased Shackley, they are still active.[6]

In this book, they're called "Not-Exactly-the-CIA."

Shackley did not believe in peace with perceived enemies, but neither did he favor a plain old-fashioned 'hot' war against them. Shackley preached what he called "the third option" – covert attacks, incessantly waged, against all perceived enemies. Especially after wide-spread public dissent against the Vietnam war while he was CIA's Saigon station chief, Shackley prized national security over open government by the people, whom he came to perceive as part of the problem.[7] He preferred a "banana-republic" form of government, which, although "elected," nevertheless crushes dissent by whatever means necessary.

PLANNING

Gene Wheaton is one of several military-investigations agents who will be mentioned in this book, each of whom over the years observed criminal covert actions by the Shackleyesque crew.[8]

The following is from an interview in which Wheaton speaks to documentary film maker Matt Ehling:

---

5   *The Third Option*

6   Under the law, a forcibly retired agent may maintain contacts he made through the agency. Outside the law – with no one watching, pretty much – an ex-agent can recruit agents still within the agency to help him, privately, for monetary gain. Unavoidably in this work, the term "CIA" shall refer primarily to a Shackleyesque crew of roguish veterans plus rogue elements still on staff. But occasionally, the term will refer to official CIA management.

7   There may have been a grain of truth in this assessment – according to Soviet defector Stanislav Lunev, during the Vietnam War the Soviet Union spent more money funding the US anti-war movement than it did on funding and arming Viet Cong forces. *Through the Eyes of the Enemy: The Autobiography of Stanislav Lunev*, Regnery Publishing, Inc., 1998.

8   Wheaton was with the US Air Force Office of Special Investigations. He had many CIA contacts. In addition, from 1985 to 1989, Wheaton was a consulting investigator on the Iran-Contra affair, briefing the staffs of the special prosecutor, the House/Senate Select Committee, and Pentagon officials.

> (I)n the late 1970s in McClean, Virginia ... Ted Shackley and Vernon Walters and Frank Carlucci and Ving West ... used to have park-bench meetings so nobody could overhear their conversations. They basically said, "With our expertise at placing dictators in power" – and I'm almost quoting verbatim one of their comments – "why don't we treat the United States like the world's biggest banana republic and take it over?" And the first thing they had to do was to get their man in the White House, and that was George [H.W.] Bush.

Although others might, I do not question that Wheaton overheard Shackley and crew saying such things. For me, the best critical question to ask of this account is, Was the "banana republic" proposal for the US made partly or entirely in jest. That is possible. But importantly, even if it was, it still plots the outline of a plan – sketching motive, means, and opportunity – to "take over" power in America.

This is important because, as we shall see in Chapter Two, this arguably seditious (even traitorous), "banana republic" proposal was not the first of its kind to be created by American government officials – U.S. Army officers, in 1976, ordered the crafting of a plan for an attack on New York's Twin Towers with airliners hijacked by men armed with plastic box cutters. Sound at all familiar?

Chapter 1

The Devil's Workshop

Below are details from a surveillance report by officers of the Indio, California Police Department covering an arms demonstration held at the Lake Cahuilla police firing range on September 10, 1981.

> The license plate number of each car that arrived on the scene was [recorded]... The Report (listed) names... of everyone who attended the demonstration [including]:
>
> Peter Zokosky: President of Armtech Coachella.
>
> Earl Brian: Wisconsin businessman and CIA employee.
>
> John D. Vanderwerker: ... CIA Research Director [for] 8 years.
>
> Two Nicaraguan [anti-Sandinista] Generals: Eden Pastora, Commander Zero; and Jose Curdel, Commander Alpha.
>
> Honduran Telephone Company Military connection network (representative) in Southern Hemisphere.
>
> Art Welmas: Tribal Chairman of Cabazon Indians.
>
> Scott Wesley: [Picatinny Arsenal] United States Army.
>
> Michael Riconosciuto: Researcher for Cabazon Indians.[1]

Riconosciuto was a researcher for the Cabazon Indian Security-Wackenhut Services Inc. joint business venture, which organized the event.

That night, the Cabazon tribe, whose reservation was next door to the firing range, hosted a "demonstration-for-sale" of weapons produced in the joint venture with Wackenhut. Dozens of sophisticated rifles were sold that night, illegally, to Contra commander Eden Pastora. CIA staffers in attendance at the event, Earl Brian and John Vanderwerker, witnessed and consented to this illegal arms sale. This behavior is enough to count

---

1   The report also mentioned unidentified Saudi princes in attendance. It is reproduced in Martha Honey's, *Hostile Acts*, University Press of Florida, 1994. An attorney, Nicholas Bua, questioned the veracity of the police report, but he lost his court case. Additionally, in a deposition in a previous court case, Contra Commander Pastora corroborated the substance of the police report. Pastora testified under oath that he saw some Saudi Arabian princes at the firing range that night.

them as members of the Shackleyesque crew, "Not-Exactly-the-CIA," described in the introduction.

This was a seminal event that would have consequences stretching forward for many years. That stretch of time is the subject of this book, beginning with background for the arms-sale event.

During the late 1970s, as we have seen, Ted Shackley and fellow zealots were conspiring in Virginia. At this time, there arose an entity called First Intercontinental Development Corporation (FIDCO). This company will be very important later in this book, and its early years are intimately associated with the Cabazon-Wackenhut joint venture.

A director of FIDCO was arms-maker Robert Booth Nichols. He and his partner in Meridian Arms, Peter Zokosky, were deemed essential by Wackenhut to the success of the Cabazon-Wackenhut arms venture. One company official wrote another,

> The obvious key to any such endeavor is [Peter] Zokosky. He is reportedly one of only 67 personnel in the world who have had any significant experience in the development and manufacture of the slurry process involved in combustible cartridge cases.[2]

In addition, Zokosky had an inside contact at the U.S. Army arsenal called Pickatinny, whose representative Scott Westley attended the firing-range arms sale described above.

A second FIDCO director, and also a director of the parent company of Zokovksy's Meridian Arms, was Clint Murchison, Jr., owner of the Dallas Cowboys football team. A third FIDCO director was former CIA agent Robert Maheu.

FIDCO was formed to take advantage of chaos in war-torn Lebanon.[3] Its board of directors also included then-assistant to President Ronald Reagan, Michael A. McManus. This status in Lebanon for the CIA-related FIDCO came about in the late 1970s, at a time when legal counsel to Wackenhut was future CIA director William Casey, and when former CIA agent Ted Shackley and cohorts were talking about making the U.S. "the world's biggest banana republic." The arms demonstration near the Cabazon Indian Reservation came soon after, in 1981, after Casey became director.

---

2   Internal memo of May 25, 1981, from Robert Frye, a Wackenhut vice president in Indio to Robert Chasen, Wackenhut vice president at the company's home office in Coral Gables, Fla. From the files of Michael Riconosciuto, obtained by journalist Cheri Seymour.

3   A corollary of Shackely's third option is that chaos is more manageable than peace.

As the surveillance report indicates, present at the arms demonstration were CIA agents Earl Brian and John Vanderwerker. On that September night, beyond offering high-tech rifles, lasers, and night goggles for sale, joint venture officials had plans to manufacture weapons using a then-secret technology. With the aid of Cabazon tribal sovereignty – an effective immunity from most U.S. laws[4] – they planned to complete another project in secret. The project was for a fuel-air explosive weapon, and FIDCO was to be involved in paying for it.

In a court deposition, Robert Booth Nichols[5] – Peter Zokosky's Meridian Arms partner – verifies that FIDCO took part in the plan for the Cabazon-Wackenhut venture to make fuel-air explosives:

> Nichols: It was '82 -- I am approximating, '82, '83, '84, that period.
>
> Q: Who paid you this money?
>
> Nichols: These funds were provided by an entity called Fedco [sic – the entity is FIDCO]
>
> Q: What did you do for F(i)dco?
>
> Nichols: I was involved with them jointly and several other parties in the development of the fuel air explosive.

The assignment to develop a secret fuel-air explosive weapon went to Michael Riconosciuto, a science prodigy and research director for the Cabazon-Wackenhut joint venture.

It should be noted that one Cabazon story, *Return of the Buffalo*,[6] casts the reservation as an innocent place in which Wackenhut simply helped an impoverished tribe and nothing secretive went on; indeed, George Wackenhut's biography, authorized by Wackenhut Corporation, omits Cabazon Indian Reservation entirely.[7]

The Wackenhut company even goes so far as to deny any association with Michael Riconosciuto. This is not believable.[8] And since Riconos-

---

4   Wackenhut memo, Ibid. at 2: "It should be noted that several key ingredients necessary for successful manufacture are available through the use of land on the Cabazon Reservation in Calif. (including) lack of opposition by adjacent governing bodies and 'irate citizens' over the siting of such a facility."

5   Dec. 16, 2008 New York Dist. Ct. for the Southern District, Case No. Cr. 1039 CT.

6   Ambrose Lane, *Return of the Buffalo*, Bergin and Garvey, 1995.

7   The Wackenhut Corporation in 1994 copyrighted a biography by John Minahan, of founder George Wackenhut titled, The Quiet American, International Publishing Group. Neither company is a traditional publisher of non-fiction. Bergin and Garvey chiefly publishes children's books. International Publishing Group offers a variety of self-published, or "mascot" works. When these books appeared, the two companies were based a golfer's stroll away from one another – on opposite sides of the Birchwood Country Club in Westport, Conn.

8   Journalist Cherl Seymour writes, "Yet in Michael's files, I found a letter written on Me-

ciuto will remain important to this story in several coming chapters, notably in his connection to FIDCO, it would be well to flesh him out at this point.

WHO IS MICHAEL RICONOSCIUTO?

To many Americans, the name Michael Riconosciuto is vaguely familiar – from the Inslaw case involving Promis software, on which we will touch in a later chapter. He is a scientific prodigy, who as a boy built a state-of-the-art laser to win a summer science camp award at Stanford University. Dr. Arthur Leonard Schawlow, a Nobel laureate Stanford University physics professor, remembers: *"You don't forget a 16-year-old youngster who shows up with his own argon laser."*[9]

Said Samuel Cohen, inventor of the a-neutronic bomb,

> I've spoken to Michael Riconosciuto and he's an extraordinarily bright guy. I also have a hunch, which I can't prove, that (he) indirectly work(s) for the CIA.[10]

In the late 1970's, the director of the National Security Agency traveled to California to visit the Riconosciuto family laboratory. The government was interested in Michael's projects, especially a hand-held "directed-energy" weapons system.

According to FBI agent Ted Gunderson, in 1979 or 1980 the CIA developed a "control jacket" for Riconosciuto, effectively pre-blackmailing him with threat of arrest as a drug pusher if he didn't cooperate fully and forever.

Michael Riconosciuto in prison

ridian Arms letterhead, dated February 10, 1984, from Robert Booth Nichols to Dr. Harry Fair (a colleague at Pickatinny Arsenal of Scott Westley's) referring to the Wackenhut visit to Pickatinny Arsenal in May 1981. Nichols reminded Dr. Fair of the demonstration there in which 'Michael Riconosciuto [had] discussed electrostatic heat transfer augmentation in a wide range of applications... and demonstrated control of heat in electric discharge.' This letter was significant in that it confirmed that Riconosciuto had in fact accompanied Peter Zokosky and Robert Frye, Vice President of Wackenhut, to the Pickatinny Arsenal to demonstrate the above-mentioned technology."

9 Wikipedia
10 Quoted by J. Orlin Grabbe on TheCatBirdSeat Web site.

A Riconosciuto court *affidavit*, Case No. 8500070, reads as follows:

> During the early 1980's, I served as the Director of Research for a joint venture between the Wackenhut Corporation of Coral Gables, Florida, and the Cabazon Band of Indians of Indio, California (that) sought to develop and/or manufacture certain materials that are used in military and national security operations, including... fuel-air explosives and biological and chemical warfare weapons.

Before leaving the FIDCO connection to Lebanon, I want to note that in the late 1970s, while Ted Shackley conspired in Virginia and Casey and Wackenhut set their sights on Cabazon – and the NSA director visited Michael Riconosciuto, a major heroin route out of Lebanon to the U.S. was established, with CIA knowledge.[11] This will be important in Chapter 8, which is related closely to this chapter.

As we shall see, this choice by Cabazon-Wackenhut venture officials to use genius Michael Riconosciuto to develop and refine fuel-air explosive weapons fits well with the warning by Shackley – who saw effective dissent against US policy as a threat to America – that his cohorts would act to "restore some control over events which threaten our very survival." This Shackleyesque gambit, the covert use of fuel-air explosives, eventually shaped future events that would simultaneously cow and stampede the U.S. population – and help rigidify America's National-Security State.

---

11   As we shall see in Chapter 8. Cf. *Time* Magazine, June 24, 2001.

CHAPTER 2

SHACKLEY AND THE PERFECT TERRORIST PLAN

Around the time of Ted Shackley's reported meetings in the park in McLean, Virginia, in 1976, the U.S. Army drafted "the perfect terrorist plan."[1] The Secretary of the Army at the time was Martin R. Hoffman.[2] The plan drawn up on Hoffman's watch was an eerie blueprint of precisely what happened to the Twin Towers 25 years later when, on September 11, 2001, a computer system in Bedford, Mass. failed to scramble U.S. fighter jets. This faulty system belonged to Mitretek, spun off from MITRE, a company run by the same Martin R. Hoffman (see Chapter 20 for analysis of this 'coincidence').

The Army's perfect terrorist plan was devised, ostensibly, to develop counter-terror defensive methods. The plan came to light in a 2003 lawsuit brought by Ellen Mariani, wife of a 9/11 decedent. In an affidavit for the suit, U.S. Army Cpl. Timothy McNiven gave disturbing details of a government project commissioned to him and some two dozen other soldiers of C-Battery 2/81st Field Artillery, stationed in Strasbourg, Germany, in 1976.[3]

Under oath, McNiven said,

> We were given the scenario of hijacking an airliner and crashing it into … a 100-story building [later specified as] the World Trade Center.[4]

For the plan, McNiven suggested use of plastic-encased box cutters to bypass airport metal detectors (first installed in 1972), his affidavit states.

He said he also recommended "having a group of passengers rush the hijackers."[5]

McNiven said,

---

1   Which we will review, and which, the record suggests, was implemented detail-for-detail on 9/11.
2   Hoffman has said he does "not recall" being involved with the plan.
3   Cf. www.markdice.com/documents/grillfire.pdf
4   McNiven affidavit, para. 12.
5   Mc Niven affidavit, para. 17.

There were people from the Defense Department and the CIA who were monitoring the study ... I wasn't able to get their names.

At this point, a good question is: What would have happened if, previous to 9/11, these facts had been widely reported?

Inescapably, the answer is that somebody would have said, "*Hey, wait a minute! We've heard about this before – in connection with the CIA and the Defense Department.*"

Understandably, Cpl. McNiven felt apprehensive while he worked on the study. He stood up, he said, and told superiors he would go public if and when the World Trade Center was ever hit with an attack matching that which he and his fellow soldiers were drawing up.[6] This enraged some in the room, who punched and pummeled McNiven, but, he said,

> [A week later] I was given the direct order that if the Twin Towers were ever attacked the way we discussed in the 1976 study, I was to do everything in my power to bring the similarities to the attention of the American people. I was told that this order was never to be rescinded, because those who would rescind it would be the very same people who turned against the American people.

On September 11, 2001, watching television, McNiven underwent a psychological and emotional ordeal. He said,

> As I watched the Twin Towers really collapse on the morning of September 11th, I realized I was watching the very same thing we devised in 1976.

To silence potential (and inevitable) critics, McNiven has successfully passed a credible lie detector test regarding both his participation in the study and the order he got to go public in case an attack on the Twin Towers in fact occurred.

Disturbing questions are raised by this Twin Towers attack scenario drawn up in 1976, with Army Secretary Martin R. Hoffman's oversight. What if the plan fell into the hands of an enemy? Spies go after such things. A contingency plan is just a blueprint – for use by enemies either foreign, like Soviets or Jihadis, or domestic, like Not-Exactly-the-CIA.[7]

---

6   Ibid., paras. 22, 23.

7   In November 2000, less than a year before 9/11, a similar contingency plan was exercised in simulation – the Pentagon Mass Casualty Project simulated a plane crash into the Pentagon.

CHAPTER 3

WACKENHUT AND MUSTARD GAS

William Casey was Wackenhut's outside attorney until 1980, during the birth of the Wackenhut-Cabazon joint arms venture. Ronald Reagan, almost certainly on firm and secret advice from powerful unknown parties, tapped Casey for CIA director.

> Former Reagan administration official Howard Teicher wrote, "(In early 1981) the CIA ... Director Casey ... knew of, approved of, and assisted in the sale of non-U.S. origin military weapons ... to Iraq.[1]"

This was all secret,[2] in part because chemical weapons were involved. Wackenhut special projects executive Bruce Berckmans, a CIA agent, said the projects included manufacture of poison gas, for export.[3]

In 1981, according to Wackenhut-Cabazon research director Michael Riconosciuto,

> The joint venture sought to develop and/or manufacture [weapons including] biological and chemical warfare weapons.

So, in May 1981, four months after the Wackenhut-Cabazon arms demonstration near the Indian reservation, several principal attendees at the arms demonstration[4] traveled to the Picatinny arsenal in Wharton, New Jersey, joined by Wackenhut vice president Robert Frye.[5] And, in Washington DC, the Wackenhut-led party met with legal experts[6] on the

---

1 Affidavit by Teicher filed in connection with a criminal trial in Miami in 1995.
2 Senator Donald Riegle, the Michigan Democrat who chaired Senate hearings on Iraq's weapons programs and Gulf War illness, concluded this in 1994. The Washington Post's Michael Dobbs, after poring through thousands of unclassified government documents, reported it in detail in a December 30, 2002, article.
3 *Spy Magazine*, 1992.
4 These included Dr. Earl W. Brian, a CIA agent; Michael Riconosciuto, CIA-asset research director for the Cabazon-Wackenhut joint venture, John P. Nichols, Cabazon tribal-finance manager; and Peter Zokosky, an arms maker. Cf. Cheri Seymour, *The Last Circle*.
5 Wackenhut internal memos secured by author Cheri Seymour., reproduced in *The Last Circle*. This group was greeted on May 12, 1981 by arsenal officials including Dr. Harry Fair – with whom Frye had been corresponding by letter. Dr. Fair almost certainly was accompanied by fellow arsenal official Scott Westley, who himself had attended the January Cabazon-Wackenhut arms demonstration held in Indio.
6 William Briggs and Glade Flake.

International Traffic in Arms Regulations (ITAR). The ITAR governs export of chemical weapons – of which a very common type is mustard gas.

Makers of mustard gas often use the chemical thiodyglycol, which also has agricultural uses. In the early 1980s, the American company, Phillips, supplied Iraq with thiodygycol but then cut off supply when Iraq ordered 500 metric tons of the chemical within one year. Phillips suspected Iraq intended to make mustard gas.[7]

That was 1984.

In ensuing years, records show, some other unidentified U.S. supplier provided Iraq with thiodygclycol; American scientists reported this after the first Gulf War, writing,

> ...produced in the United States, and illegally diverted from their intended recipients, [drums of thiodiglycol] were found by international inspectors after the Gulf War at Iraqi chemical-weapons production sites.[8]

The record also shows that the thiodyglycol arrived in Iraq via the Nu Kraft shipping company,[9] with whom a man named Frans van Anraat reportedly worked, while van Anraat was an informant for the Dutch intelligence agency, AIVD.[10] At this time, the CIA was recruiting AIVD for help in destabilizing Soviet border republics.

Researcher Cees Wiebes writes,

> The fact that the Dutch Intelligence Services participated with the CIA in these operations is now clear to me.[11]

No records appear to exist which identify the company that used Nu Kraft to ship its TGD product to Iraq. That suggests the identity of this company is a kept secret. What does the record also suggest toward identifying this company?

One venture that was secret and wanted to profit from chemical-weapons manufacture was the Cabazon-Wackenhut joint arms venture (pre-

---

7   Edward Spiers, *Chemical and Biological Weapons: A Study of Proliferation*, Macmillan Press Ltd., 1994. Iraq then ordered amounts of other mustard-gas precursors, but these shipments were intercepted by U.S. agents at the docks, and never arrived.

8   Federation of American Scientists Web site.

9   Johnathan Tucker, "Trafficking Networks for Chemical Weapons Precursors: Lessons from the Iran-Iraq War of the 1980s," Monterey Institute of International Studies, 2008. In April 1988, a U.S. Customs sting in Baltimore uncovered a shipping network – the companies Nu Kraft and Alcolac working together – that in 1987 and 1988 shipped 635 tons of thiodyglycol to Iraq.

10   Reported in the *Volkskrant*, a 250,000-circulation Dutch newspaper, December 2004.

11   Intel Today Web site September 2, 2016. Wiebes is Senior Research Fellow at the Ad de Jonge Institute for Intelligence and Security Studies.

viously discussed in Chapter 1). Reportedly, Iraq was using mustard gas until 1991.

In that context, Journalist John Connolly gives the following account:

> [Six months before the first Gulf War], in the winter of 1990, former Marine Corps sergeant David Ramirez, 24, a member of the Wackenhut Corporation's Special Investigations Division, known as founder and chairman George Wackenhut's 'private FBI,' a unit that provided executive protection and conducted undercover investigations and sting operations was sent with three other members of SID to San Antonio. Once they arrived, they rented two cars and drove four hours to a desolate town on the Mexican border called Eagle Pass.[12]

In Eagle Pass in 1986, Wackenhut opened a private "detention center" in conjunction with the U.S. Border Patrol. Eagle Pass also houses the sprawling Laughlin Air Force Base. During the 1980s and beyond, a Wackenhut security company held a contract for the Laughlin base.[13]

At the time, the Laughlin base had been used for decades for "secret operations," including CIA-sponsored flights of the U2 reconnaissance plane over Cuba.[14] And GEO Group, a private-prison corporation begun by Wackenhut, currently has a facility in Eagle Pass.

The facts above demonstrate that Wackenhut held a position of power in Eagle Pass, through contract relationships with Laughlin AFB and the Border Patrol, which, as the two largest Eagle Pass employers, dominate the town. Wackenhut's capacity for "black ops" at Laughlin has often been utilized by the CIA.[15] It would have been unsurprising, indeed it would have been a characteristic fit, for activities of the Wackenhut-Cabazon arms venture to have been carried out, with CIA cover, in complete secrecy at some remote corner of Laughlin AFB. This includes chemical-weapons manufacture.

In this context, let us rejoin author Connolly's narrative of Sgt. Ramirez and the other Wackenhut SID agents' appearance just after dark at Eagle Pass:

Connolly recounts that, upon arrival, the four senior Wackenhut security men met two truck drivers near a warehouse. Inside the warehouse, the Wackenhut men said, was a big rig, an 18-wheel tractor-trailer. The Wackenhut men were instructed to convoy the rig in secret to Chicago.

---

12   John Connolly, "Inside the Shadow CIA," *Spy Magazine*, September 1992.
13   Porch.com Inc. Web site.
14   Wikipedia.
15   "It is known throughout the industry," says retired FBI special agent William Hinshaw, "that if you want a dirty job done, call Wackenhut."

The security men were armed with shotguns, but Wackenhut told them nothing about the cargo.

> "My instructions were very clear," Ramirez recalls. "Do not look into the trailer, secure it, and make sure it safely gets to Chicago."[16]

The Wackenhut truck made for and found the Pan-American Highway, Interstate 35, northbound. During fuel stops on I-35 in a drive of 30 hours, Wackenhut men parked close alongside the big rig. They kept a shotgun in easy reach in the open mouth of a car trunk, Connolly recounts from his interview with Sgt. Ramirez.

On the third day, after departing from I-35 onto I-80 eastbound, around 5 a.m., the Wackenhut men delivered the trailer to a "warehouse outside Chicago."

Wackenhut never identified the cargo. Ramirez didn't ask, but his curiosity grew. He kept considering, he said,

> ... the secrecy, the way the team was assembled in a remote location, and the orders not to stop or open the truck.

Wackenhut eventually offered Ramirez the explanation that it was U.S. Food Stamps, worth millions, the company said, on which he had ridden shotgun from Texas to Chicago. Connolly writes,

> Ramirez decided he didn't believe that explanation. Neither do we. One reason is simple: A Department of Agriculture official simply denies that food stamps are shipped that way. "Someone is blowing smoke," he says. Another reason is that after a six-month investigation, in the course of which we spoke to more than 300 people, we believe we know what the truck did contain – equipment necessary for the manufacture of chemical weapons – and where it was headed: to Saddam Hussein's Iraq. The Wackenhut Corporation was making sure Saddam would be getting his equipment intact.

Connolly's sources for this story, excepting Sgt. Ramirez, declined to be identified.

In conclusion, the record suggests that it was the Wackenhut-Cabazon arms venture whose thiodyglycol component for mustard gas reached Iraq via shipment by the Nu Kraft firm at a time when Nu Kraft was represented by a Dutch AIVD intelligence informant, and when the CIA and AIVD were working together in destabilizing Soviet border repub-

---

16   Ibid. to 12.

lics. The reported gassing of Iraq's Kurdish dissidents counts as a modern American disaster – a war-crime for private profit – in which the U.S.'s rogue intelligence community, including Wackenhut and the rest of Not-Exactly-the-CIA, was involved.

CHAPTER 4

PROMIS

Also around 1976, while Ted Shackley et alii were talking about a "banana-republic takeover" of the U.S. government and Martin R. Hoffman's soldiers were drafting a 'hypothetical' plan in which airliners attacked the Twin Towers, a newly invented computer software, Promis, was proving to be versatile beyond the dreams of its creators, Bill Hamilton of the National Security Agency and his wife, Nancy Hamilton. The Hamiltons' Prosecutor's Management Information System (Promis) could cross-reference multiple data bases, crunching everything ever recorded digitally on a criminal suspect, with which package, updated constantly, cops and district attorneys could "see" the status of

Bill and Nancy Hamilton

a suspect – where he was staying, his associates, even his habits. The Hamiltons founded the INSLAW company around their invention of Promis.

It became evident to government agents that the versatile Promis could "track" and give "status-updates" not only on low-level criminals but also on high-scale movers of stock holdings, arms, and drugs. It could track anybody – potential operatives, informants, etc. Thus, Promis was even more valuable to the spy community than it was for law enforcement. As was publicized in the INSLAW court case, the Promis super-software was stolen from the Hamiltons around 1982 – with a court verdict eventually holding that it was the U.S. Justice Department itself who had stolen Promis. The record suggests strongly that the thieves, while indeed government-connected, were not prosecutors but rather intelligence agents.

Foreign intelligence agencies, such as Syria's, bought the modified Promis from CIA agent Earl W. Brian, who attended the Cabazon-Wackenhut arms demonstration, and from British Mossad agent Robert Maxwell.[1] Thus the official CIA *and* Not-Exactly-the-CIA could view what Syria's secret service

---

1   *The Mirror,* UK, "British Publisher Robert Maxwell Was Mossad Spy," December 6, 2002.[4] As ex-CIA agent Victor Marchetti put it, "The Agency would hire Satan himself as an agent if he could help guarantee the national security."

(MID), say, had on a particular Arab – where he was, whom he'd seen, what he'd been doing, especially what dirty or illegal things he had done. NE-CIA could then find, say, a Mr. Habib, could lean on him with dirt they'd eavesdropped, and extort his services, or buy his fighting services.[2] Agents could also buy names of other possible recruits, and the real CIA, through Promis, could most likely find and buy them too, and so on, until a large network of fighters and other operatives was under contract and close surveillance via the tracking software. This describes resources available for the official CIA covert operation to arm the Afghani Mujahideen in their fight against the Soviet Union in the early 1980s.

There was always potential for parallel uses of Promis by the unofficial but affiliated Not-Exactly-the-CIA. Technically non-existent, NE-CIA needed to raise its own operating money, as did the CIA itself frequently, to supplement its official budget. Promis could track the international black market, which put agents in position to take cuts of profits from drugs-for-arms sales they could easily have stopped. For example, Col. Oliver North told Israeli officials in December 1984 that he planned to use profits from future arms sales to support the Contras.[3] Before that, in Laos, Ted Shackley and the CIA's infamous Air America helped maintain, and took profits from, the local opium/heroin network.[4]

To modify the stolen Promis for use by spies and those in their world, CIA agent Earl W. Brian hired Wackenhut-Cabazon's researcher, science prodigy Michael Riconosciuto. The modification Brian wanted was a "back-door" capability for Promis software, by which any computer running this modified Promis software could be hacked, taken over surreptitiously, and used for clandestine purposes.[5]

As we shall explore further later on, many banks were lured into buying the modified Promis, and, through it, were turned into unwitting money laundries.

Bill Hamilton told author Cheri Seymour that, based on his experience as an NSA agent, he believed,

> Riconosciuto's job was to help (the Contras and the mujahideen) avail themselves of NSA's bank surveillance version of Promis to launder the proceeds from the drug sales.[6]

2   *New York Times*, November 19, 1987.
3   Intercept.com Web site, May 12, 2018
4   Spartacus Educational Web site; also cf. *The Politics of Heroin in Southeast Asia*, Alfred McCoy, Lawrence Hill Books, 1972.
5   Riconosciuto court affidavit in INSLAW case, 1991; cf. *Washington Post*, "Key Witness in Justice Dept. Software Case Jailed," March 31, 1991.
6   Seymour, *The Last Circle*, p. 65.

Evidently, U.S. news outlets were slow to grasp the scope, and the potential for nefarious use, of the Promis software, but a few stories did hint at this.

The *Washington Times* on June 14, 2001, reported "software likely in hands of terrorist." *Newsweek*, on Sept. 23, 2002, reported that the Reagan administration in the 1980s had allowed sales to Iraq of computer databases that Saddam Hussein could use to track such diverse matters as movements of political opponents and shipments of "bacteria/fungi/protozoa" (which could help produce anthrax and other biological weapons). Not much else was written on the topic in the U.S. media.

But Canadian intelligence officials, early on, smelled a cyber-rat. They suspected their Promis software, bought from Earl Brian, was back-door modified and that the CIA thus had secret access to Canadian government computers. Royal Canadian Mounted Police came to the U.S. and looked for proof.[7]

Mounties Sean McDade and Randy Buffam were helped by American private detective Sue Todd, who was from the Riconosciuto family's company town of Hercules, Calif., and by American investigative journalist Cheri Seymour. Seymour had access to Riconosciuto's personal records of his clandestine work, which he kept because he was always afraid his CIA handlers would arrest him in order to silence him. Writes Seymour,

> The Mounties gained a clear picture of the men with whom Riconosciuto associated, including mob figures, high-level government officials, intelligence and law-enforcement officers and informants – even convicted murderers.[8]

This is a good partial description of Not-Exactly-the-CIA.[9]

The modified Promis could also track aircraft flight plans, and at its Bedford, Mass. air-control site, from which computers governed air response to 9/11, the FAA hired a contractor, MITRE, that used a program termed by experts as "very like" the modified Promis; its "twin." At the time of the 9/11 attacks, Martin R. Hoffman, former Secretary of the Army, was running Mitretek, a company indistinguishable, except on paper, from MITRE. Hoffman – the man who seems to have forgotten that in 1976 (as mentioned in Chapter 2), he oversaw the U.S. Army's drafting of the perfect terrorist attack: hijacked airliners striking the World Trade Center.

---

7   *Insight* magazine, October 31, 2006.
8   Seymour, *The Last Circle*.
9   In Hercules, Calif., CIA agent Earl Brian's Bio-Rad Company acquired land surrounding the plant of Riconosciuto's family company, Hercules Manufacturing. Brian's Bio-Rad spinoff, Hadron, would figure in the anthrax scare after 9/11 (see Chapter 16).

CHAPTER 5

FUEL-AIR EXPLOSIVES

Around the time of the Soviet invasion of Afghanistan in 1980, both the U.S.S.R. and the U.S. were at work refining a formidable weapons technology – the fuel-air explosive (FAE).

By 2000, Russia had used a highly refined version of FAE against Chechen separatists.

Researcher Lester W. Grau of the U.S. Army Foreign Military Studies Office describes fuel-air explosive as follows:

> Fuel-air weapons work by initially detonating a scattering charge within a bomb or rocket warhead. The warhead contents, which are composed of either volatile gases, or liquids, or finely powdered explosives, form an aerosol cloud. This cloud is then ignited, and the subsequent fireball sears the surrounding area while consuming the oxygen in this area. The lack of oxygen creates an enormous overpressure ... 1.5 to 2 times greater than the overpressure caused by conventional explosives.... Personnel under the cloud are literally crushed to death. Outside the cloud area, the blast wave travels at some 3,000 meters per second. The resultant vacuum pulls in loose objects to fill the void. As a result, a fuel-air explosive can have the effect of a tactical nuclear weapon, without residual radiation.[1]

The first combat use reported of FAE explosive was in the early 1980s, by Soviet troops, in Afghanistan's Panjshir Valley.[2] U.S. possession of the FAE technology at that time apparently was a government secret, because no news reports of that time mention it. An FAE firestorm is eerie, apparently like nothing ever seen before. Commenting on this weapons technology, proponents have always noted its power to terrify.[3]

---

1   "A 'Crushing' Victory: Fuel-Air Explosives and Grozny 2000," Lester W. Grau, Timothy Smith, *Marine Corps Gazette*, August 2000.
2   Ibid.
3   "(FAEs) were used by the United States in Iraq during Operation Desert Storm. A total of 254 CBU-72s were dropped by the United States Marine Corps...They were targeted against mine fields and personnel in trenches, but were more useful as a psychological weapon....The CBU-72 consisted of three fuel-air explosive (FAE) sub-munitions. Each sub-munition weighed about 100 pounds and dispensed a cloud approximately 60 feet in diameter and 8 feet thick composed of its 75 pounds of ethylene oxide aerosol fuel across the target area, with air-burst fusing set for 30 feet. An embedded detonator ignited the cloud as it descended to the ground to produce a mas-

It was invented in the late 1960s. According to declassified government documents viewed by former FBI agent Ted Gunderson, in the early 1980s Wackenhut officials contacted science prodigy Michael Riconosciuto to develop an FAE known as the "electro-hydrodynamic gaseous fuel bomb" for the Wackenhut-Cabazon joint arms venture.

Working in secret in the early 1980s at the laboratory of his family company, Hercules Manufacturing, Riconosciuto developed a type of FAE he nicknamed "Blue Death."

In 1983, the CIA's Dr. Earl W. Brian, through his Bio-Rad company, bought the property on which Riconosciuto's Hercules Manufacturing laboratory sat. In 1985, a company called Dyno-Nobel acquired the Hercules Manufacturing company itself. Dyno-Nobel and the CIA thus would have acquired Riconosciuto's "Blue Death" FAE technology.

In a U.S. government contract dating from 1990, the Dyno-Nobel company was tasked to produce fuel-air explosives for the military. This led indirectly to a secret being revealed: America possessed FAE technology.

In 1994, the U.S. Department of Energy's Office of Non-Proliferation and National Security conducted something called The Non-Proliferation Experiment (with "proliferation" short for "proliferation of nuclear weapons"). The experiment was, ominously, designed to produce a non-nuclear explosion that packed destructive power equal to some nuclear weapons – a bomb, in other words, whose use would not attract horrified attention by spreading nuclear radiation.

Some American reporters got an earful while covering an April 1994 gathering called the "Symposium on Non-Proliferation Experiment (NPE) Results and Implications for Test Ban Treaties." Reporters heard results of NPE tests conducted by Dyno-Nobel earlier that year at the US government's Nevada Test Site, a secret location patrolled by Wackenhut, the company that hired Riconosciuto to produce his "Blue Death" FAE refinement – the electro-hydrodynamic gaseous fuel bomb.

Presenting test results at the symposium, Mark Mammele of Dyno-Nobel said,

> The requirements of the Non-Proliferation Experiment, as outlined in the original explosives bid package, presented Dyno-Nobel, Inc., with a unique challenge. The size of the [detonation] chamber, the total volume of explosives required, the chemical-energy equiv-

---

sive explosion. The high-pressure of the rapidly expanding wave front flattened all objects within close proximity of the epicenter of the fuel cloud, as well as causing debilitating damage well beyond it. Like other FAE using ethylene oxide, in the event of non-ignition, it functions as a chemical weapon, due to the highly toxic nature of this gas." Globalsecurity.org Web site.

alent of 1 kiloton, the time-frame of loading the chamber, transportation, and safety were all necessary considerations in choosing
this particular explosive.

It was not reported that this particular underground test, almost certainly of Riconosciuto's Blue Death FAE, lowered the ground level at the
Nevada Test Site by 30 feet.[4]

A year later, some researchers suspected fuel-air explosives were used
in the Oklahoma City bombing. Riconosciuto at that time acknowledged
his belief, based on details of the OKC incident, that the weaponry used
was of his design – the Blue Death FAE. Even so, Riconosciuto was never
accused of participating in the OKC bombing. This, likely, was because
at the time he was still a valuable "intelligence" asset, a member in good
standing of Not-Exactly-the-CIA.

---

4   According to FBI agent Ted Gunderson.

CHAPTER 6

THE STRATEGY OF TERROR

In 1940, Edmond Taylor's book, *The Strategy of Terror*, detailed how the French population was being persuaded to remain largely docile under Nazi rule.[1] This was done by inculcating fear of the Soviet Union and Bolshevism.

After World War II, with the Germans and Japanese successfully defeated, the U.S. itself, led by hard-right Republicans, turned on the old bogeyman of Socialism and deployed vigorous propaganda – claiming the Soviets and international Communism intended to rule the planet. The record indicates American intelligence agents effectively crafted a domestic Strategy of Terror and applied it to the U.S. population beginning early on in the Cold War. The work of anti-communist zealot Sen. Joe McCarthy and his House Un-American Activities Committee began a powerful era of red-baiting in early 1950, but a decade later, McCarthy was discredited, and fear of the Soviets was waning as the two superpowers, following the "Spirit of Geneva" arms talks in 1955, tentatively pursued nuclear détente. Something new was needed, for zealots of the McCarthy stripe, to recharge anti-communist hysteria.

German anti-Bolshevik poster distributed in wartime France.

TWA FLIGHT 529

On May 1, 1960, the CIA sent Captain Gary Powers on an ill-fated spy flight over the Soviet Union in a plane known as U2. The incident caused allegations, even within the U.S., that the CIA had downed the plane to kill nuclear détente between the U.S. and the U.S.S.R.

---

1 Edmond Taylor, *The Strategy of Terror*, Houghton-Mifflin, 1940.

University of Delaware professor James Nathan put it strongly, saying,[2]

> The anomalies in the Powers case suggest that the U2 incident may
> have been staged.[3]

Senator William Fulbright opened senate hearings on the U2 flight,
saying,

> No one will ever know whether (the U2 downing) was accidental
> or intentional … I have often wondered why, in the midst of these
> efforts by President Eisenhower and Khrushchev to come to some
> understanding, the U2 incident was allowed [by the CIA] to take
> place.

On the 11th of May 1960, in a long-planned move of détente suddenly
tainted by the U2 incident, American nuclear scientists began an historic
tour of Soviet nuclear labs, which was followed two months later by five
peace-minded Soviet physicists touring nuclear facilities in the U.S., including the Argonne National Laboratory, scene of the subsequent crash
of TWA 529. But, U2 had killed détente. A year later, on August 31, 1961
– the day before a nuclear moratorium lapsed – the Soviets announced
they would resume bomb testing.

That evening, in Lemont, Indiana, residents near the Argonne National Laboratory ate dinner, likely watched the announcement on television
that the resumption of nuclear testing was "Soviet terror,"[4] and began a
night's sleep. Three hours later, an explosion shook them from their beds
as TWA Flight 529 blew up and crashed – near the atomic-weapons laboratory. The population was terrified.

"Dear God, what is this – the bomb?" a Mrs. Rehak[5] said she thought
to herself.

"It sounded like an atomic bomb," householder Charles George said.

"I thought the Argonne Laboratory had blown up," said a local police-
man, who saw flames in the sky.

---

2   J. Nathan, article in "Military Affairs" (1975) published during the Senate Select Committee on Intelligence investigation into CIA assassination plots.
3   Powers's final account, according to London Times journalist John Judge, was that the
U2 plane lost altitude due to what Powers believed was sabotage on the part of the CIA – a move to
undermine the possibility of nuclear detente between Eisenhower and Khrushchev. Not long after
giving that account, in August 1977 veteran pilot Powers was dead in a civilian helicopter crash, supposedly out of fuel. Many believe he was murdered by the CIA to keep him from talking about U2.
4   New York Times Chronology - John F. Kennedy Presidential Library …(1:8; Text, p. 4, August 31, 1961
5   Gendisasters.com Web site. This Web site uses sources including Illinois' Edwardsville In-
telligencer, 1961-09-01.

TWA 529 exploded one minute short of striking the nuclear laboratory. An FAA crash report ruled, "accident."

No one survived the crash. The odds weigh heavily against this for an accidental crash.[6] Also suspect is the fact that the official passenger list for TWA Flight 529 printed not only names but also home towns for all passengers except one – Robert Gordon.[7]

According to the *Hammond* (Indiana) *Times*,[8] passenger Gordon purchased a ticket from the Hoosier Motor Club at Indianapolis and arrived in Chicago aboard an Eastern Airlines plane, destination San Francisco. The Hoosier Motor Club said Gordon gave a Bloomington address on the University of Indiana campus.

However, the *Hammond Times* continued, the university said Gordon was a graduate student at a University of California campus, and had come to Indiana for a conference with a botany professor, Dr. Richard Starr, with whom Gordon had studied in the previous summer on a project at a Woods Hole, Massachusetts research station.

This research station was the U.S. government nuclear submarine warfare laboratory at Woods Hole Oceanographic Institution, whose researchers during World War II gathered classified information for amphibious landings and anti-submarine warfare. In short, from his work there, Gordon likely had some sort of government security clearance – in addition to a home-town situation sketchy enough that TWA, going against airline policy, did not declare one for Gordon on the Flight 529 passenger list.

On September 1, 1961, the day that the nuclear moratorium lapsed – with the Soviets having declared they'd resume testing – at 1:18 a.m. Central Standard Time TWA Flight 529 arrived at Chicago's Midway Airport. The plane sat on the tarmac for 42 minutes before taking off again. During this time, passengers got on and off, as did flight crews – pilots and attendants – creating a shuffle in which a bomb could have been put on the plane by someone who never rode the plane. Robert Gordon, say, might have been among those on board when 529 took off, and died with others when the plane crashed, but since victims' bodies were burned beyond recognition, there is no proof of this.

In light of these facts, and in the context of media hubbub about "Soviet terror" and the fear on crash day that an American nuclear laboratory had come under attack, there is sufficient reason to suspect a false-flag attack

---

6   In the United States, between 1983 and 2000, there were 568 plane crashes. In 90 percent of these there were survivors.

7   GenDisasters.Com Web site, citing the *Pittsburgh Press.*

8   September 1, 1961.

was done on TWA 529 as part of a strategy of terror by intelligence-community Americans against the U.S. populace.

CHAPTER 7

THE QUEEN'S ACCIDENT, 1983

In early March 1983, Queen Elizabeth of England attended Ronald Reagan's wedding anniversary party in San Francisco. From there, the Queen was escorted to Yosemite Valley. In between those points, east of the foothills town of Mariposa, a car collision occurred – known as "The Queen's Accident" – between a sheriff's vehicle and a Secret Service car.

The Mariposa County Sheriff's Office at the time was under media scrutiny. The department was widely believed to have covered up the suspected murder of Deputy Ron Van Meter, who had alleged fellow deputies off-loaded drug shipments at night from planes at Mariposa County Airport. An internal investigation into the alleged corruption and the death of Van Meter, led by Sheriff's Sgt. Rod Sinclair, Jr., was widely dismissed as incomplete and fraudulent.

This was the context in which the Queen's Accident occurred, and it was Sgt. Sinclair's car that the caused the crash.[1] An unidentified San Joaquin County official told Sacramento reporter Jerry Goldberg, "The fatal accident which occurred to Queen Elizabeth's escort vehicle ... is related to [the ongoing Mariposa County corruption]."

FACTS

The Queen's Accident occurred when Sgt. Sinclair's car swerved at high speed and struck an oncoming Secret Service vehicle, killing three agents in the Queen's escort. Besides the Queen's limousine, the only vehicles on the road belonged to the Sheriff's Department or the Secret Service, and without question the two agencies had coordinated before the royal entourage arrived.

Sylvia Emery, a lifelong dweller in Mariposa, said residents asked, "How could it have happened?"

No definitive answer has come to that question.

After the crash, a bomb was found in Sinclair's trunk. Reporters couldn't ask Sinclair about it – because his attorney managed to set a gag

---

1   A court ruling split the blame 70-30 between Sinclair and a Secret Service driver.

order.[2] The bomb apparently disappeared into thin air and has never been mentioned again. No charge was ever brought against Sinclair. As such, this bomb's technology very likely was of a sensitive nature – a secret that needed keeping.[3] This profile fits a fuel-air explosive, which at the time was a secret defense technology proprietary to the CIA.[4]

The record shows that in the months preceding the accident, Sgt. Sinclair had been a man badly frightened of something connected to his past. He had booby-trapped his yard with bombs, according to fellow Mariposa deputy Rod Cusic.

The question arises with the gag order, the CIA-imposed secrecy in the Queen's Accident, and Sinclair's yard full of bombs – what might Sgt. Sinclair have known that was sensitive/secret, federally, and needed protection from the public? Sinclair was addicted to Demerol, a tongue-loosening painkiller.[5] What did Sinclair know that, stoned on Demerol, he might have blabbed?

For example, Sgt. Sinclair did know of a secret spy-training program run in post-war Japan by his father, Army Col. Rod Sinclair, Sr., and sponsored by Gen. Douglas MacArthur. Having lived in Japan with his father, Sinclair Jr. knew a spy trainee named Harold Okimoto – a Yakuza criminal.[6]

Writes author Cheri Seymour, "I had privately mused how many of MacArthur's men later became arms of the Octopus."[7]

HAROLD OKIMOTO

Internal Wackenhut correspondence from December 1982 and January 1983 shows that Wackenhut-Cabazon joint venture officials discussed a bioweapons manufacturing operation[8] to be run by Meridian Arms (Mi-

---

2   Thenceforth, reporters couldn't ask Sinclair anything about corruption in the Sheriff's Department. The issue was virtually killed for the next 18 years, until ABC's *20-20* reported it, on November 15, 1991.

3   And something about the Mariposa corruption was also related to the same people who secreted the bomb.

4   As we have seen, Not-Exactly-the-CIA takes steps to control persons who know too much. A good example is Michael Riconosciuto, whom NE-CIA fitted with a "cover jacket" – of "drug maker" – under which the government jailed Riconosciuto in 1991.

5   Interview by Cheri Seymour with Shaula Brent, one of Sinclair's medical providers, *The Last Circle*, p. 25.

6   By strict tradition, Japanese spies were culled from the Yakuza, a criminal-cum-benevolent organization.

7   By "the Octopus," Seymour refers to a term coined by investigative reporter Danny Casolaro, in an unpublished work interrupted by his death by murder or suicide. For the group of this nature, other names coined have included "The Secret Team," coined by U.S. Air Force Col. L. Fletcher Prouty, and my "Not-Exactly-the-CIA."

8   Wackenhut internal memos obtained by Riconosciuto and from him by author Cheri Seymour.

chael Riconosciuto was an officer of Meridian Arms). A director of its parent, Meridian International Logistics (MIL), was Harold Okimoto.[9]

According to Cheri Seymour, Wackenhut official Robert Chasen shut down a Cabazon bio-weapons project that was producing a bio-agent "with horrendous properties."[10] This likely happened in early 1983. At around the same time, Okimoto and MIL illegally transferred rights to a U.S. government *bio-weapon* project to Japan.[11]

Through Okimoto's former trainer Col. Rod Sinclair Sr., details on MIL's transfer to Japan of bio-secrets, and on other illegal covert operations by NE-CIA, were privy to Sinclair's son, a drugged, loose-tongued Sgt. Rod Sinclair, Jr. As such, it is quite conceivable the "Queen's Accident" collision was designed to kill the younger Sinclair.

Okimoto, working as he did for deputy CIA director Frank Carlucci, was in the loop on Not-Exactly-the-CIA at a pivotal time – the inception of NE-CIA in the late 1970s, marked by the seemingly related events described below.

COVERT DIRT

Between 1976 and 1980, in the milieu of a "cowboy" CIA under pressure by Jimmy Carter and spawning, as a result, its freelance satellite group, NE-CIA, the following events occurred that characterize the birth of NE-CIA:

1. After training by Col. Rod Sinclair Sr., Harold Okimoto worked under deputy director of the CIA Frank Carlucci, a soon-to-be Wackenhut board director.[12]

2. Carlucci met secretly on a park bench with disgruntled CIA agent Ted Shackley to discuss a "banana-republic" takeover of the U.S. government (see Introduction).

3. Upcoming CIA director William Casey worked as an attorney for Wackenhut.

4. The Wackenhut-Cabazon joint weapons venture began, with Contra arms supply as an objective.

---

9   Another was Eugene Giaquinto, who also directed the parent of Yosemite Park and Curry Company in Mariposa County during an FBI probe of drug dealing there.

10   *The Last Circle*, p. 161

11   Norio Hayakawa Web site, February 19, 2016: Corporate minutes of MIL, dated August 26, 1988, along with signed agreements, revealed that biological technology labeled "The Method for Induction and Activation of Cytotoxic T-Lymphocytes" was handed over to the Japanese for further research.

12   Wikipedia.

5. A drug operation run by ex-police officers and ex-intelligence agents, known as The Company, flourished out of Fresno to fund the Contras.[13]

6. Mariposa County Dep. Ron Van Meter was murdered, allegedly by fellow deputies on whom he blew the whistle for drug dealings out of Mariposa County Airport.[14]

Keeping secrecy for all of this together is more than enough to warrant a severe control measure by Not-Exactly-the-CIA, such as the "Queen's Accident," against Sgt. Sinclair, burying a corruption investigation under a controlled non-investigation of a spectacular occurrence: a fatal crash involving a Queen's escort.

AS MARIPOSA RESIDENTS ASKED, HOW COULD THE COLLISION HAVE HAPPENED?

Obviously, the Queen's travel through Mariposa County qualified for the utmost in coordination between the Sheriff's Office and the Secret Service.

But after the crash, dazed and injured, Sinclair kept asking, "Where did they come from? Why were they in my lane?"[15]

It was agreed in court that the Secret Service driver had been "straightening out" bends by crossing the median line. Sgt. Sinclair, for his part, had been speeding at around 64 miles per hour on a winding road. Obviously, each driver involved in the crash had reason to believe he could safely drive the way he did. Where did this belief, this assurance come from? It could only have come from briefings of the Secret Service driver by a federal commander and of Sinclair by a Sheriff's commander – likely Sheriff Paul Paige.

---

13   The Company had been written up in the *San Francisco Chronicle* on April 28, 1982 under the heading "Story of Spies, Stolen Arms, and Drugs." According to reporter Bill Wallace, The Company "possessed planes, ships, and lots of real estate… Federal drug agents said the organization had imported billions of dollars' worth of narcotics from Latin America, and was also involved in gunrunning and mercenary operations."

When investigator Cheri Seymour asked Michael Riconosciuto who was behind the Mariposa County drug/corruption ring, Riconosciuto said,

> "The Company. Arms get shipped to the Contras, the Afghanistan rebels (mujahideen)…to fight the Soviet influence. But the Contras and Mujahideen don't have money to pay for arms, so they pay with drugs, cocaine or heroin. The Company handles the drug end of it in the US…."

14   An ABC 20-20 reporter asked Mariposa Sheriff Paul Paige whether drugs were being flown into Mariposa County Airport for a large ring to transport for sale in California metropolitan areas (the reporter did not mention Contra funding, but that issue was a heated one at the time). Paige scoffed.

15   Web site Auto Week, by Paul Kayfetz, attorney-at-law

It was Sheriff Paige who in 1980 made Sgt. Sinclair the chief investigator of the death of whistle-blowing Deputy Ron Van Meter and of the surrounding airport-drug corruption controversy. Even after evidence emerged in 1990 that Van Meter had been murdered, Paige publicly pooh-poohed the idea of drug transports at the county airport, much less a cover-up murder. This makes Paige suspect as a helper in keeping the complex web of Not-Exactly-the-CIA secrets described listed above (in items 1 through 6).

An instruction by Paige to Sinclair to speed on his way back, coupled with federal instruction to the Secret Service okaying to line-cross, would have just about guaranteed a high-speed, head-on collision. With that, if Sinclair lived, a lawyer could silence him with a gag order, which is in fact what happened.

In the aftermath of the Queen's Accident, besides a bomb of some kind, fully-automatic, military-style rifles were discovered in Sinclair's vehicle. No information was ever forthcoming on how these illegal weapons came to be in Sinclair's trunk. Under a gag order, Sinclair never denied nor confirmed publicly whether he had put them there.

No information has ever been given about what type of explosive was found in Sinclair's car. This does not prove, but certainly doesn't rule out, the bomb being a fuel-air explosive, which, in the 1980s, was proprietary to the CIA. This in turn would have meant immediate CIA unofficial control of the entire investigation, and of all media releases, pushing aside the FBI. Conveniently, just then in 1983, an agent named James Kallstrom was rising in FBI ranks. As we shall see in Chapter 9, Kallstrom apparently enjoyed playing welcoming mat for the CIA (and its satellite NE-CIA) to take control, *sub rosa*, of FBI cases.

CHAPTER 8

GANDER

Two years after The Queen's Accident, on December 12, 1985, an airline crash at Gander, Newfoundland, killed 256 people, most of them U.S. soldiers. Many witnesses said they believed a crime was involved. Eventually, U.S. officials ruled it was just a tragic accident.

On Arrow Airlines Flight 1285, the soldiers were coming home from Cairo, Egypt, after occupying the Sinai Peninsula under the 1979 Camp David Accords between Egypt and Israel.

Under these accords, President Jimmy Carter pledged to ship $3 billion in arms to Cairo.[1] The shipper selected turned out to be a front for the Egyptian national intelligence agency – the Central Security Forces (CSF)[2] – and skimmed $8 million off its government contract.[3] This was EATSCO (Egyptian American Transport and Security Co.), an offshoot of a company founded by Ted Shackley, in a clear iteration of Not-Exactly-the-CIA.

In the Sinai, the Shackley-allied Central Security Forces were nearly all-powerful. Agents used travel checkpoints to control movements of people and goods, including opium, on the Peninsula. Ostensibly, this supervision of drug-running was done in exchange for intelligence information from smugglers,[4] who frequently spoke English and tended to know people's activities. But, as cited by journalist Mark Perry, a private American intelligence agent testified before the European Union, "The Sinai is flooded with contraband...and a lot of that comes right out of CSF pipelines."[5]

In this environment, then, U.S. Army forces were deployed. Attached to the 101st Airborne Division in Sinai was Special Agent Dirk Miller of the Army's Criminal Investigation Division (CID). Miller had the job of

---

1   *Washington Post*, October 9, 1982.

2   According to CIA agent Edwin Wilson and EATSCO founder Hussein Salem, cited in *New York Times*, September 6, 1981.

3   Ibid. to 1.

4   In 1985, Israeli tourist Tsur Shezaf saw much drug use in Sinai resort towns. Asking around, he heard of the following: "(F)ive drug rings... According to former operators of these networks, three (drug rings) were operated by Israeli intelligence and two by Egyptian intelligence."

5   Mark Perry, "Looking for Hashish in Cairo? Talk to the Police," Aug 23, 2013, Foreign Policy.com Web site.

investigating persons "with a nexus to" the military,[6] a group that included U.S. intelligence agents. U.S. spies in Sinai at the time were largely obliged – by language barrier and by unfamiliarity with the territory – to work alongside Egyptian CSF agents. Because this constraint put U.S. "military-nexus" people right alongside CSF's business of monitoring opium transport from the hills to the coast, part of Miller's duty had to have been watching for undue involvement in the opium trade by CIA agents, ex-CIA agents, and other nexus-to-military people.

Evidently there was a substantial population of such agents in Sinai at the time that distinctly bore watching.

BACKGROUND

Under the Camp David Accords, Cairo in 1985 was both mecca and haven for spies, ex-spies, and arms dealers. In this milieu, the shadier among these men formed Ted Shackley's API Distributing, a "petroleum-services company." Then, born from API was the interlocked Egyptian American Transport and Security Company. EATSCO's front man was wealthy Cairo entrepreneur Hussein Salem, and in its background were the Shackley cronies Edwin P. Wilson and Thomas Clines, both CIA agents. During this time, Ed Wilson also had a contract with Syrian arms dealer Monzer al Kassar.[7] From the early to mid-1980s, Not-Exactly-the-CIA was gathered in Egypt in force.

Keeping an eye on and busting these freebooters – for the $8 million EATSCO arms fraud – were Army CID investigators who preceded Dirk Miller. EATSCO officials got off with fines, and Not-Exactly-the-CIA was free to continue its staple business of taking cuts of drugs-for-arms profits.[8] NE-CIA's only obstacle in Sinai in 1985 was the continued presence of Army CID investigators, now spearheaded by Agent Dirk Miller.

In this context, then, Miller was positioned to observe – and the record suggests he did observe – the CIA-CSF supervision of drug-running in Sinai. Miller was scheduled to file reports to his superiors upon his return to the United States. Miller's reports likely would have led Army brass into a public showdown with the CIA on Sinai in particular and on drugs-for-arms in general.

---

6   An Army CID memorial to Dirk Miller states, "(Special Agent) Miller… provided expert guidance and criminal investigative support to Task Force 3-502 (101st Airborne)."

7   Al Kassar would figure largely in the story of the 1988 bombing of Pan Am 103 (see Chapter 9).

8   Shackley's crew continued suspect arms sales in the region through the coming years, according to Thomas Clines's working associate, CIA Agent Glenn Robinette. Cf. *New York Times*, June 18, 1987.

Publicity would have blown the lucrative Sinai arms-drugs operation for Not-Exactly-the-CIA participants. The record suggests NE-CIA
members were aware of the threat Miller embodied and that they acted to
remove it. Miller's home-bound plane, Arrow Air 1285, was bombed, and
Miller died aboard.

A cover-up ensued that, as reported by Army CID investigators, involved U.S. secret agents. As investigative columnist Jack Anderson wrote
four years after the crash,

> A former Pentagon investigator [Army CID agent] has relentlessly
> gone after what he thinks is a "cover-up." His private crusade has
> become so public that in August the outgoing chairman of the Joint
> Chiefs of Staff, Adm. William J. Crowe Jr., asked a top Army attor-
> ney to find out what the investigator knew. [9]

Anderson relates that an associate of his heard "well-placed sources"
(which almost certainly means the above-referenced CID investigator)
describe actions of "covert operatives, who were neck-deep in secret arms
sales to Iran."

These covert operatives, the Anderson source said, covered themselves
by claiming to have found that a soldier on Miller's flight had accidentally
detonated a hand grenade, causing the crash. Jack Anderson wrote,

> Our sources claim the grenade story was a hoax to persuade the
> Army to cooperate in a cover-up of anything that would point to-
> ward an [criminally caused] explosion.

The Arrow Air company has a sketchy history. Arrow Air was a "son"
of the CIA's proprietary Air America, formed after Congress forced its
termination. Air America had ferried arms into and opium out of Laos
during the Vietnam War under the direction of our ubiquitous CIA agent
Ted Shackley.[10]

How plausible is it that Shackley's group of hyper-patriot cowboys[11]
killed 256 people to assassinate Miller? For ex-Army intelligence agent
Gene Wheaton, who worked closely enough with Shackley and cronies to
overhear an arguably treasonous conversation they had on a park bench
(see Introduction), the answer is "fully plausible." In an interview with
documentary film maker Matt Ehling:

9   *Washington Post*, November 9, 1989.
10   Alfred McCoy, *The Politics of Heroin in Southeast Asia,* Lawrence Hill Books, 1972.
11   Shackley was the CIA agent who wrote "I am not alone" among thousands of forcibly retired agents determined to keep doing hard-core anti-communist operations after Jimmy Carter's
election; see Introduction.

"The covert operators that I ran with would blow up a 747 with 300 people to kill one person," said Wheaton. "They are total so-ciopaths with no conscience whatsoever."

The fact that Arrow Air 1285 crashed in Canada allowed the FBI to drop all responsibility for a probe, claiming its only role *was to* help iden-tify bodies. It fell to the Royal Canadian Mounted Police to investigate. They were suspect, however, in their capability. At the time, the RCMP was in a shambles. It had just been torn apart and partially replaced by a new agency, the Canadian Security Intelligence Service, for illegal 1970s cowboy-like operations paralleling CIA behavior of the time (which prompted President Jimmy Carter to tear apart the CIA in 1980 by firing thousands of agents, including Ted Shackley). For example, anti-commu-nist zealots in the RCMP had blown up a suspected meeting place be-tween Front for Liberation of Quebec leftists and American members of the Black Panther Party, after a judge refused a warrant request on the property.[12] And going back as far as 1969, a tear-down of RCMP was al-ready proposed, but the RCMP protested it had "built up meaningful li-aison with security services and police forces in foreign countries which could not be readily acquired by a new service." This was at the height of, for example, Shackley's murderous CIA-cowboy Operation Phoenix in Vietnam.

Not long before Gander, according to several accounts,[13] the RCMP illegally bought stolen Promis software from the CIA's Earl W. Brian – modified with a secret back door by Michael Riconosciuto. It is likely that RCMP operations at the time of the Gander probe were being quietly monitored by Not-Exactly-the-CIA.

NE-CIA had the ability and motive to tell its fellow "cowboys" in the RCMP how to handle the Gander crash investigation, and, through the secret back door in Promis, Brian's and Shackley's people could check to see that the Mounties followed their lead. With the FBI not investigating Gander, RCMP's work would become the sole basis for the now largely dismissed verdict of – "icing-on-the-wings."

A few years after the crash that killed CID agent Dirk Miller, the Not-Exactly-CIA crowd from Egypt would show up in Lebanon and the nearby island of Cyprus. There, with CIA asset Michael Riconosciuto, they operated under the now-familiar aegis of FIDCO (First American

---

12   *Macleans*, December 8, 2006.
13   By CIA assets Robert Booth Nichols and Michael Riconosciuto, and Israeli military intelli-gence agent Ari Ben Menashe.

Development Company), which in Indio, Calif., had paid Riconosciuto and arms dealer Robert Booth Nichols for development of fuel-air explosives, as part of the Cabazon-Wackenhut joint arms venture.

CHAPTER 9

LOCKERBIE

Three years after the Gander crash of Arrow Air Flight 1285, Pan American Flight 103 was destroyed in a bomb explosion above Lockerbie, Scotland. As of this writing, over 30 years after the crash on December 21, 1988, an appeal is pending on a criminal conviction of Libyan Abdelbaset Megrahi. Legally, nothing is resolved about who bombed the plane.[1]

Mainstream news accounts of the crash agree that a bomber somehow made use of a heroin sting operation by the DEA involving air flights traveling from Lebanon to the U.S.[2] As we saw in Chapter 1, Lebanon was a sphere of operations for an American outfit called First Intercontinental Development Corporation (FIDCO) that in the early 1980s managed Michael Riconosciuto as he modified the Promis software and refined fuel-air explosive technology for the joint arms venture between the Cabazon Indians and Wackenhut Services, Inc.

LEBANON AND FIDCO

In the late 1980s, almost certainly via Promis, Riconosciuto tracked movements of people in Lebanon. Said Riconosciuto, "FIDCO (First International Development Corporation) had a companion company, called Euramae Trading."

Euramae owned a house offshore from Lebanon, in Nicosia, Cyprus. This is where Riconosciuto and DEA agent Lester Coleman worked, and where Coleman said he observed crates labeled "PROMISE." The DEA used the house for a so-called sting operation. Coleman said the Euramae-FIDCO house was a job-related hangout for DEA and CIA around a so-called drug sting, adding,

> [M]embers of the Jafaar clan and other DEA couriers would arrive at Larnaca [Cyprus] with suitcases full of high-grade heroin, white and crystal, and be met off the boat... by officers of the Cypriot Police Narcotics Squad, who then drove them up to the Euramae office in Nicosia.[3]

1   The government of Libya has paid reparations to victims' families, but this seems largely or wholly to do with escaping from under U.S. sanctions against Libya, a condition of the payments.
2   Cf. *Time* magazine, June 24, 2001.
3   Lester Coleman & Donald Goddard, *Trail of the Octopus*, Bloomsbury *Publishing* PLC,

According to NBC, as part of the so-called "sting," the next leg for the heroin was by air, from Nicosia to Frankfurt, Germany. There (with DEA sanction) heroin was loaded on airliners bound for the U.S., all operated by Pan American Airlines.

NBC-TV News reported the following:

> Including (Flight) 103 ... *Pan Am* flights from *Frankfurt* had been used a number of times by the DEA as part of its undercover operation to fly informants and suitcases of *heroin* into *Detroit* as part of a sting operation to catch dealers in *Detroit*.[4]

That is, as journalist Bill Weinberg reported,

> The CIA and DEA had apparently both instructed German's intelligence agency, the BKA, to allow certain suitcases to pass uninspected onto US-bound (Pan Am) flights at the Frankfurt airport, where Flight 103 originated.[5]

Pan American 103 was flying Frankfurt-to-London-to-New York. Suitcase inspectors for the flight, as was customary in a "sting," would have passed the usual heroin suitcase. But, in addition that day, it is likely that these bribed inspectors were employed to pass a second suitcase, containing a bomb, onto Pan Am Flight 103.[6]

DEVIL'S WORKSHOP EAST – RE-ENTER MICHAEL RICONOSCIUTO AND THE PROMIS SOFTWARE

This so-called alleged DEA drug sting was run from the Euramae house. The heroin route involved was established by Syrian arms dealer Monzer al Kassar,[7] who three years previous had been an arms-dealing partner in Cairo with EATSCO principal Edwin Wilson.

In the autumn of 1988, a CIA team was still working with Al-Kassar in Frankfurt, Germany, according to a report prepared by former Israeli Mossad officer Juval Aviv, head of New York City-based Interfor.

Before and after Ted Shackley's time with the agency, CIA staff has included many "straight-arrow" agents, possessed of conscience, who deplore rogue activity. One such agent figures in the Lockerbie case: Beirut Deputy Station Chief, Matthew Gannon.

1993.
4   October 30, 1990.
5   *High Times*, March 1993, by Bill Weinberg.
6   It has been speculated that an Arab infiltrator of the drug "sting" gave such a second bomb to baggage handlers, but there is no evidence for this.
7   *Time* Magazine June 24, 2001.

MOTIVE

Rogue CIA agents collaborating with al Kassar for profit had good reasons to kill Gannon and his fellow Beirut operative, U.S. Army Major Charles McKee, a criminal investigator for the Defense Intelligence Agency. CIA rogue agents' sponsorship of al Kassar was illegal, and Gannon and McKee not only had discovered it, but also intended to publicly expose it.[8]

Ex-CIA director George H.W. Bush was elected president in November 1988, only 6 weeks previous to the Lockerbie bombing. Bush's years as CIA director, 1976-1977, spanned the time when al Kassar was solidifying his international drugs-and-arms operation, as was made obvious to Bush by a drug conviction in Britain for al Kassar in 1977.[9] In the wake of the Iran-Contra hearings of 1987, a large sector of the US public was highly suspicious of Bush, who later would be revealed as "in the loop" (a fact he denied at the time) for the covert and illegal Iran-Contra arms-for-hostages deal.[10]

At the time of the Lockerbie bombing, the inauguration of Bush as president was just 4 weeks away. Because of Iran-Contra, it was obvious Bush would face hard public scrutiny during his presidency. Military-investigations agent Gene Wheaton has noted that those conversations he overheard in the late 1970s between Ted Shackley and Frank Carlucci about a "banana-republic takeover" of the US government stressed the necessity of first getting "their man" (Bush) into the presidency, and obviously Shackley and Carlucci wanted that presidency to be unfettered by public scrutiny.

The record suggests a strong possibility that NE-CIA arranged the Lockerbie bombing, for two "good" reasons:

1. To protect from public scrutiny the agency's sponsorship of drugs-for-arms deals (from which it could gather intel and money) by murdering Gannon and McKee.

2. To quash American dissent and scrutiny against Bush by amplifying fears of Arab terrorism.

---

8   *Time* Magazine's April 27, 1990, cover story, written by veteran correspondent Roy Rowan. As a ranking DIA officer, McKee filed a formal complaint with the CIA. The agency failed to respond.

9   Jonathan V. Marshall, *The Lebanese Connection*, Stanford University Press, 2012.

10   G.H.W. Bush personal diary, 11/5/86: "On the news at this time is the question of the hostages ... I'm one of the few people that know fully the details, and there is a lot of flak and misinformation out there. It is not a subject we can talk about." Diary publicized in November 2015 by Fox News.

This supposition is lent credence by the recorded facts that the official CIA obstructed the Lockerbie crash investigation by covering up crucial information and by introducing false testimony.

INVESTIGATION AND LEGAL PROCEEDINGS: A CIRCUS OF CONCEALMENT

A British official has said of the Lockerbie case, "No court is likely to get to the truth now that various intelligence agencies have had the opportunity to corrupt the evidence."[11]

Private investigator Juval Aviv's Interfor company was hired by Pan American Airlines after it was accused of negligence in the deaths of passengers. Defense attorney Gareth Peirce gleaned the following from the Interfor investigation report:

> [S]cores of men, some wearing no insignia, some the insignia of the FBI or Pan Am [it was noted at the time that many of these men were clearly not Pan Am staff], invaded the area.[12]

THE MEBO MUDDLE

It is now widely acknowledged that tainted evidence was introduced in the case, much of which appears to have arisen through rogue CIA agents exploiting a Swiss company called Mebo, which made timers.

Mebo Telecommunications, Inc. employed a key prosecution witness, Ulrich Lumpert, an engineer. Lumpert confessed to helping corrupt the Lockerbie investigation.

In an affidavit of July 18, 2007, Lumpert wrote,

> I confirm ... that I stole the third hand-manufactured MST-13 Timer PC-Board consisting of 8 layers of fiberglass from MEBO Ltd. and gave it without permission on 22th June 1989 to an officer of the Swiss federal police (BUPO).[13] It did not escape me that the MST-13 fragment shown [at the Lockerbie trial] on the police photograph No. PT/35(b) came from the nonoperational MST-13 prototype PC-board that I had stolen.

---

11   Former British Ambassador to Libya Oliver Miles.
12   Gareth Peirce, "The Framing of al-Megrahi," *London Review of Books*, September 24, 2009. Attorney Peirce said that to bolster its case the defense could point out that Thomas Thurman, the FBI forensic expert responsible for the Pan Am 103 investigation, was forced out of the FBI after a Justice Department inquiry found that he had allowed examiners in his explosives unit to overstate conclusions in favor of the prosecution in several cases. Peirce is a British defense lawyer who has represented a number of people threatened with extradition to the United States.
13   Mebo Telecommunications AG Web site.

The Swiss officer handed it over to Mr. Alan Feraday[14] from [Britain's RARDE, Royal Armament Research and Development Establishment].

The Swiss BUPO officer referred to by Lumpert is Peter Fluckiger, according to an interview with Lumpert in June 2008 by WordPress blogger[15] Matt, who reports,

> On June 6, 2008, Lumpert told me that he gave a MST-13 timer prototype to Swiss Commissioner Peter Fluckiger. According to Lumpert, Fluckiger requested this device and other material at the demand of a "friendly Intelligence Agency."

This "friendly" intelligence agency was the CIA, according to George Thomson, who on WordPress July 21, 2016 said he'd found a Swiss government document confirming this.

Meanwhile, in England, Alan Feraday's defense agency RARDE was given, by police, a fragment of a timer ostensibly found at the crash site of Pan Am 103. RARDE and the FBI elaborately traced this fragment to Mebo manufacture, but RARDE never tested the fragment for explosive residue, which would have supported or dismissed the Semtex-explosive theory.[16] Why not?

RARDE "had not been able" to test the fragment, testified John Douse, then a forensic scientist with RARDE, because of "cost savings at the laboratory."[17] This, in the deadliest air disaster in British history, in 1988, when Britain's defense budget, including funding for RARDE, was around $25 billion (£19 billion).[18] No, something besides thrift likely caused RARDE's failure to make the crucial test for Semtex.

The operation to corrupt evidence needed help from both Swiss agent Peter Fluckiger, whom Lumpert names, and from Jordanian agent Marwan Khreesat. Their help was needed to plant the theory that Semtex was used in the Lockerbie bombing. Prosecutors used circumstantial evidence to argue the explosive was Semtex; and used that theory to obtain the conviction of *Abdelbaset al-Megrahi*, a Libyan.

---

14   Feraday was key in introducing a fake thread about Malta in an initial prosecution attempt to pin the bombing on Libyans.

15   *New York Times*, May 20, 2012. Note that I offer blogposts only when, from other sources, I can lay a firm foundation for what a blogpost reports; they are the new journalism, after all, and offering them with a corroborating source seems the best approximation that can be made of traditionally standard journalistic attribution.

16   *New York Times*, May 20, 2012.

17   Reuters news agency report appearing June 5, 2000 on the South African IOL website.

18   Hansard record of British Parliamentary debates, 26 January 1988.

According to lead case investigator, FBI agent Richard Marquise,[19] on October 24, 1988, Jordanian intelligence agent Khreesat was working against the Palestine Liberation Organization in the German city of Neuss, near Frankfurt. The record suggests Khreesat entrapped Hafez Dalkamouni, a Palestinian, into being found in possession of Semtex.

Going shopping in Dalkamouni's car, the pair was surveilled by the German intelligence agency BKA, which had been tipped by Khreesat (BKA is the same agency the CIA cooperated with to employ Pan Am baggage handlers to pass particular suitcases on board uninspected).

Two days after the surveillance, BKA agents stopped Dalkamouni's car with Khreesat as passenger and reportedly found an alarm clock modified to make a time-delay firing device, and Semtex plastic explosive. In subsequent raids at Palestinian houses in other cities, tipped again by Khreesat, BKA also found Semtex and clocks. In the public mind, news stories effectively linked a relationship between "Semtex," "timers," and "Palestinians."

With this setup, rogue CIA agents could make full use of manipulating the timer company, Mebo.

In the aftermath of the Lockerbie crash, Mebo co-owner Edwin Bollier was interviewed at the CIA training center in Quantico, Virginia.[20] Bollier recounts the following:

> I was offered by Task Force chief Richard Marquise a sum of up to US $4 million if I would sign a police protocol stating that [Mebo] MST-13 timer fragment PT/35 (allegedly found at Lockerbie) was part of a 20-piece delivery of MST-13 timers from Mebo to Libya.

The record shows other witnesses were CIA-bribed. On October 2, 2007, the *Herald Scotland* reported, "The CIA offered $2 million to the Crown's key witness in the Lockerbie trial and his brother, sources close to the case have told the *Herald*."

In July 2018, British government departments blocked a scheduled release of documents pertaining to the Lockerbie investigation because, the government said, publicity on them would either undermine foreign relations or impinge on national security, or both.[21]

---

19   FBI agent Richard Marquise, *Scotbom: Evidence and the Lockerbie Investigation*, Algora Publishing, 2006. Marquise led the U.S. investigation of the Lockerbie bombing.
20   Edwin Bollier, from Mebo Telecommunications Web site, April 2012. His interview shows the CIA was obviously in charge of the US Lockerbie "investigation," despite the FBI's Richard Marquise being titular head of it.
21   UK *Daily Mail* July 28, 2018.

MEANS

The means of the Lockerbie bombing is still in dispute as of this writing.

A witness to the explosion told a TV interviewer,

> There was this absolutely massive sort of red glow in the sky that went firstly upwards and then out. We thought it was some sort of nuclear explosion.

But no radiation evidence exists for a nuclear bomb.

And if it wasn't Semtex or a suitcase nuke, it almost had to be a fuel-air explosive to pack the punch that the bomb had – the punch of a small nuclear device – which is fuel-air explosive's trademark. This detail brings us back to Nicosia, Cyprus, the first stop out of Lebanon for heroin bound for Frankfurt, illicit loading onto Pan American flights, and on to New York City.

Working at the FIDCO/Euramae Cyprus office in 1988 was "technical advisor for FIDCO"[22] Michael Riconosciuto. As we saw in chapter 1, science prodigy Riconosciuto was the FIDCO crew's go-to-guy for fuel-air explosive expertise.

So, if required by NE-CIA handlers at the FIDCO/Euramae house in Cyprus, Riconosciuto was available, in December 1988, to do a readiness check on a fuel-air explosive device.

OPPORTUNITY

Such a fuel-air explosive device could easily have been suitcased at the Euramae house, couriered by Cypriot police to be taken aboard a Nicosia-to-Frankfurt flight – a procedure already routine at Euramae with heroin suitcases – and at Frankfurt routinely put aboard Pan Am 103 by CIA/BKA-employed handlers working the so-called drug sting.

To sum up, if publicity on reports from Matthew Gannon and Charles McKee on CIA complicity in heroin-running had ever hit the newsstands, it likely would have caused complete upheaval in the US intelligence system, among Shackley's rogue veterans, active staff agents, and high officials – just after an ex-CIA chief, G.H.W. Bush, had been elected president. In comparison to this prospect, considering who probably did the judging, it might well have seemed perfectly justified to murder Gannon and McKee, along with 268 fellow humans (or 'collateral damage'), using a fuel-air explosive; thereby preserving 'Order' in government (of the

---

22   Cheri Seymour, *The Last Circle.*

G.H.W. Bush 'New World' variety), making the American people, for fear of Arab terror, unwitting accomplices to murder.

Keep Covering Up: Silence CIA Asset Michael Riconosciuto

The theory that a rogue group in and around the CIA arranged the Lockerbie bombing is also lent credence by the fact that Michael Riconosciuto was silenced soon after.

Riconosciuto moved to the State of Washington in 1990. Soon after, the DEA reassigned to Washington the federal agent who had bossed the Euramae house from which illegal sales of bootleg Promis software were made to Arab countries – Michael T. Hurley.

In 1991, nine days after Riconosciuto gave an affidavit to the inventors of Promis to help them sue the government for stealing the program, he was arrested for allegedly running a drug lab – his old "control jacket" profile from years earlier, clapped on him by the CIA to maintain his full cooperation, forever.

Says the DEA's Coleman,

> (T)he arrest of Riconosciuto should be regarded as suspect … (T) he probability is that Hurley was reassigned to Washington State to manufacture a case against Riconosciuto – in order to prevent Riconosciuto from becoming a credible witness.

This suspect jailing of Michael Riconosciuto served to silence him for more than 25 years – and counting.

Although the above record indicates Riconosciuto was released in June 2017 from California's Lompoc federal prison, a blog report suggests that either Riconosciuto may have been re-arrested only weeks later or never have, in fact, been a free man after leaving Lompoc.

Nokio Hayakawa, in a Civilian Intelligence Web site posting of July 30, 2017, wrote,

> A hero to some, Michael Riconosciuto was finally released from prison on June 27, 2017. His whereabouts now, however, is still a mystery… (H)is name was taken off the inmates' list. However, according to a source, temporarily he relocated to Nevada, and now he's back in jail in Nevada. And, according to the source, now they want to move him to Washington DC, which will be not be a good prospect for him.

CHAPTER 10

WORLD TRADE CENTER, 1993

A bomb exploded in the World Trade Center's underground garage on February 26, 1993, killing six people. Announcing this,
in a headline in 216-point type, 3 inches high, the *New York Daily
News* shouted "TERROR." The letters "T-E-R-R-O-R" occupied around
one-fourth of the News's front page.

Just 4 weeks earlier, Bill Clinton had been inaugurated as President.
Clinton had to drop everything and respond, in a national telecast originally scheduled to discuss his economic program. Clinton opened the
telecast by saying,

> Before I talk with you about our economic program this morning,
> I want to say a word to the good people of New York City and to
> all Americans who've been so deeply affected by the tragedy that
> struck Manhattan yesterday.

Not much more than an hour previously, the *Daily News* had appeared
on newsstands. A freshly inaugurated president, with big plans to boost
the national economy, was forced to address a traumatic terror event.

He needed citizens to clear their minds of the freshly sparked miasma of fear and loathing, in order to focus rationally on details of the national economy and a plan to improve it. It is not likely that many were able to do so.[1] In coming months, it was more likely for Americans to anxiously seek for reports on the threat of terror attacks[2] than to look rationally for economic progress along the lines proposed by the president.

Less than three months after the bombing, the *New York Times* ran a piece on Hillary Clinton, questioning, in an odd manner, her integrity (see Chapter 17 to follow).

Later, after 9/11, House Committee on Homeland Security chairman Rep. Michael McCaul (R-Tex.) would assess that, with the WTC 1993 bombing, the CIA took control away from the FBI forever on domestic-terror investigations. McCaul said, on the 20th anniversary of the 1993 WTC bombing,

> Coming a few weeks after President Clinton's swearing in ... the 1993 bombing of the World Trade Center ... was a tipping point in what would become a new type of war against the evolving threat of terrorism. Before the attack ... our intelligence community [was] not fully engaged ...[3]

This "engagement" of the CIA in domestic terror probes had been planned long before. In 1984, a secret powwow occurred among dozens of intelligence agents from around the world. Spies from the CIA, NSA, Defense Department intelligence, U.S. Secret Service, and intel agencies from England, Israel, and Italy met to decide whether the World Trade Center was vulnerable to terrorist attack.[4] This consortium advised intelligence agents of the New York and New Jersey Port Authority, owner of the land under the Trade Center.

The goal of the spy powwow, according to the Port Authority's Peter Caram,[5] was to develop "an expertise [for investigating domestic terror] unmatched in the United States." Clearly this meant "better than the FBI." That is, the run-up to the WTC attack nine years later was clearly meant to be a period during which the FBI was to be groomed out of the domestic-terror investigation field and replaced by intelligence officials.

---

1   This predicament prefigures the 2016 election, in which voters were bombarded with anti-Hillary Clinton Facebook posts in an operation using the research of Cambridge Analytica.
2   It still is.
3   *New York Daily News*, February 26, 2013.
4   James Glanz & Eric Lipton, *City in the Sky*, Times Books, 2003.
5   Head of the Port Authority's Terrorist Intelligence Unit.

But, due to CIA funding in the 1980s of Mujahideen fighters in Afghanistan, and the eventual results, it was only a matter of time before an Arab CIA operative turned up in a terror case. Sure enough, a prime suspect in the 1993 Trade Center bombing was Ramzi Yousef, who had fought the Russians with the Mujahideen during the '80s.[6]

Yousef rented a room in the Little Egypt quarter of Jersey City, New Jersey, with Mohammad Salameh. Salameh was later convicted of performing the Trade Center bombing.

Also implicated in the WTC bombing was Egyptian immigrant Emad Salem, from Cairo, the city that, in the early 1980s, was controlled by Egypt's intelligence agency CSF – while CSF and CIA-affiliated EATS-CO skimmed $8 million from a U.S.-to-Cairo arms shipment contract.[7] Reports journalist Peter Lance,

> (Emad Salem) was a serious player in Cairo in the 1980's, a "go-to guy" who could arrange anything for anyone – from a private tour of the Pyramids of Giza to a backstage meeting with the lead belly dancer at The Hilton. He lived the Egyptian high life... [8]

Salem, who rose to the rank of Major in the Egyptian Army, was also touted as a bomb-making expert. With all this, then, CIA men stationed in Cairo clearly would have known of and cultivated Salem. Salem migrated to the US in 1987. It is likely the CIA sponsored his relocation.

After that, in New York City, Salem worked, officially, for the FBI. Wearing a wire, Salem was assigned to surreptitiously record conversations among a clique of Muslims that attended a particular mosque.

However, Salem, with his recorder, taped his FBI handlers, too.[9]

The *New York Times* obtained these tapes and published a blockbuster story implying the FBI could have prevented the WTC blast.[10]

> Law-enforcement officials were told that terrorists were building a bomb that was eventually used to blow up the World Trade Center, and they planned to thwart the plotters by secretly substituting harmless powder for the explosives, an informer said after the blast.

---

6   *Newsday* reported, April 16, 1995, "FBI officials also are considering a probe of whether the CIA had any relationship with Yousef (who masterminded... the 1993 World Trade Center bombing)."

7   Skimming US arms money via EATSCO

8   Peter Lance, "Salem: The Man Who Risked His Life for America," based on reporting Lance did for *Playboy* magazine; Peter Lance Web site.

9   According to defense attorney William Kunstler in an interview five months after the WTC was bombed. Television station WBAI, New York City, August 3, 1993.

10   Internet search of the phrase "FBI could have prevented the WTC blast" brings up the story immediately.

The informer was to have helped the plotters build the bomb and supply the fake powder, but the plan was called off by an FBI supervisor who had other ideas about how the informer, Emad Salem, should be used.[11]

The sole "FBI supervisor" able to call off this plan would have been Agent-in-Charge James Kallstrom. As a result of scandal provoked by this news story, the *Times* evidently came under pressure, most likely from federal agencies whose goodwill was necessary for the *Times* to stay in business.

Reporter Jon Rappoport on, The News Doctors Web site, August 2, 2014, wrote:

> Several years after reporter Blumenthal wrote the above piece, I spoke with him … and wondered whether the *Times* had continued to investigate the scandal.
>
> Blumenthal wasn't pleased, to say the least. He said I misunderstood the article. Again, Blumenthal told me I "didn't understand." He became angry and that was the end of the conversation.

The FBI originally ordered a fake bomb. This order was countermanded, likely by Kallstrom. So, a real terror weapon was detonated in the Trade Center. After that, Kallstrom was in charge of both the criminal investigation and all press releases about it.

Kallstrom immediately announced that "Middle Eastern terrorists" were culprits in the bombing. Within hours, sensationally, Mohammad Salameh, roommate of the CIA-connected Ramzi Yousef, was arrested, based on the phone number of Josie Hadas, landlord of Salameh and Yousef. Evidently, Hadas was a "probable Mossad agent."[12] This phone number was found on a rental slip for a truck that Salameh rented, though Salameh said Hadas told him to rent the truck for a moving job. In Hadas's own apartment (not in the Salameh-Yousef apartment), explosives were purportedly found.

On March 5, 1993, the *New York Times* reported, "[Federal officials] declined to say who (Hadas) was – or whether she played any role in the case."

Hadas was never traced, apprehended, questioned, or implicated in the crime. That is, the FBI under Kallstrom did not go after Hadas. A compelling reason for that would have been the CIA's need for close rela-

---

11   *New York Times*, October 28, 1993.
12   Britain's *Guardian Weekly*, March 14th, 1993.

tions with Israel's Mossad. Bringing Hadas to trial, subject to under-oath scrutiny, is something the CIA would have pressured the FBI, and/or the seemingly willing agent Kallstrom, to studiously avoid.

In Chapter 12, we will discuss what happened to TWA flight 800 after taking-off from JFK Airport on July 17, 1996, the plane exploded at 16,000 feet and plunged into the Atlantic Ocean, killing all 230 passengers and crew. The FBI's James Kallstrom was in charge of investigating that crash, too. Kallstrom's probe, and predictable conclusion of equipment malfunction, drew a tremendous amount of criticism, with cover-up alleged by dozens of critics spanning the political spectrum. As usual in such matters, their cries still echo down the halls of justice, with no reply but, "Case closed."

CHAPTER 11

OKLAHOMA CITY – APRIL 19, 1995

Immediately after the Oklahoma City bombing, Ted Shackley was heard to say, "Now wouldn't you find it interesting if you found out it was terrorists from here?"[1]

On this tale of horror, the standard, well-known story is that one simple, mammoth fertilizer bomb, masterminded and assembled by Timothy McVeigh with sidekick Terry Nichols, left 169 people dead inside the gutted Fred P. Murrah Building on Fifth Street in Oklahoma City. The standard story does not mention windows blown out 16 blocks away, or cars burned along Fifth Street many yards from the building, or the firm statements of witnesses who heard more than one explosion. This standard story does not mention that McVeigh's truck was parked a full 20 yards from the Murrah building.

It is remarkable that this story ever got traction and held. Even before it was written, some of its parts were undercut by government documents and live TV footage generated immediately after the bombing. "Multiple bombs found at the site" was reported in a DoD Atlantic Command Memo, a FEMA Situation Report, and a US Forces Command Daily Log. TV crews on the Murrah site after the explosion filmed bomb-squad members carrying out an unexploded bomb from the wreckage.[2]

How was this story, the real story, suppressed? By threats.

Journalist J.D. Cash of the *McCurtain County Gazette* tried to interview members of the fire department, the bomb squad, and the police. He couldn't. Cash was generally told by potential interviewees,

> We've been told not to talk about the devices [note the plural case].[3]

Told by bosses, presumably, who'd also been *told* to put it in a bottle, by someone with the credentials and clout to sway a fire chief, a police chief, and a bomb-squad director. But Cash also reported some safety officers told him,

> –I saw a lot that day I wish I hadn't.

> –I have a wife, a job, a family. I've been threatened.

---

1   David Hoffman, *The Oklahoma City Bombing and the Politics of Terror*, Feral House, 1998.
2   KFOR Channel 4 and KWTV Channel 9.
3   May 26, 2003, from Website 100777. Recovered through WayBackMachine Website.

Someone with both the credentials to pull rank on a police chief *and* the personal presence to scare a police officer by threatening his family. Whoever it was, it was someone who can reasonably be suspected of planning the massacre.

And in fact, after a year, this very suspicion found evidence to support it. On March 20, 1996, a leaked Pentagon study dubbed Timothy McVeigh a stooge, not a mastermind.

> Sources close to the Pentagon study say Timothy McVeigh did play a role in the bombing, but peripherally, as a "useful idiot."[4]

McVeigh was, apparently, a willing fall guy; presumably for the same people who yanked the chains of the police and the fire chiefs and scared their officers – into silence.

A Closely Groomed Fall Guy

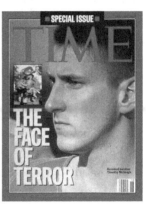

McVeigh's pre-arrest history is highly compatible with his role as a "useful idiot" in the bomb plot, especially a terror plot hatched by Not-Exactly-the-CIA. Why? Why murder 169 men, women and children? For McVeigh, rage against the machine that he felt had betrayed him. For the real puppet masters, to inoculate the American public with the idea of terror attacks on US soil – and thereby reap the benefits of more support for, and less scrutiny on, actions of national security officials – as this *Time* magazine cover intimates.

In late 1991, soon after McVeigh left the Army, he was offered a job at Burns International Security Services in Buffalo, New York, a company similar to Wackenhut Security, staffed with ex-FBI agents. A report on the company states,

> The business of Burns often necessitated clandestine or covert operations.[5]

---

4   *Strategic Investment Newsletter* March 20, 1996. It is at least somewhat likely that this "Pentagon study" was one that analyzed data found by Army *Criminal Investigation* Command (CID) agents probing "crimes by military or by persons with a nexus to the military," CID's mission area, just as the CID, including Special Agent Dirk Miller, had done in Egypt before the Gander crash.

5   FundingUniverse.com Business Histories Web site. Tellingly, Burns in December 1994 hired one Ali Mohamed, who previously had spied for the CIA and was implicated in the WTC 93 bombing by Peter Lance, "Ali Mohamed: al Qaeda Master Spy & the Feds' best kept secret"; this information was also reported in Lance's book, *Triple Cross*, Harper Collins, November 2006.

At its customer locations, Burns employed spies – posing as everything from professors to janitors. It offered fake-student spies to work college campuses, and when exposed, Burns blamed it all on a "misguided" single operative – a fall guy.[6]

Burns's client Calspan, McVeigh & Dr. Jolly West

In his job for Burns, McVeigh, was paid with CIA money. In order to reach McVeigh, the money went first to Cornell University's "Society for the Study of Human Ecology," often referred to simply as a front organization for the CIA, to distribute funds for covert research in the use of hallucinogens such as LSD[7]; and historically identified with William Thetford, a CIA contract psychologist who headed the agency's MK-ULTRA SubProject 130 until his retirement in 1980.[8]

From the Society at Cornell University, which was the contract base of the CIA's "Human Ecology Fund," CIA money went to an offshoot of Cornell Aeronautical Laboratory, a defense contractor called Calspan.9

All that remained was for McVeigh to go to the CIA money. And he did, in 1992, when Burns International assigned McVeigh to a guard's job at the former Cornell Aeronatics Laboratory, then named Calspan, on the Cornell University campus.

Why would the CIA, or NE-CIA, have wanted McVeigh employed at that particular location? The answer seems to be somewhere in Cornell's connection to a psychiatrist named "Jolly" West, a specialist in hypnosis who, at Cornell, did grant-funded Top-Secret-level contract work for the CIA on MK-ULTRA Subproject 43.[10]

West

In funding West's MK-ULTRA work, CIA grant-makers relied on two published papers by West, "Psychophysiological Studies of Hypnosis and Suggestibility" and "Studies of Dissociative State."[11]

---

6   FundingUniverse.com Business Histories Web site.

7   Glenn E. Tagatz, "Enigma: a Veteran's Quest for Truth, XLibris, 2013; Peter Conners, *White Hand Society*, City Lights Books, 2010

8   Wikipedia.

9   Alex Constantine, *Virtual Government*, Feral House, 1997.

10   West was known as the Maestro of Mind Control and was chosen by Ronald Reagan and the CIA's Dr. Earl W. Brian to run a so-called violence-study center in California that allegedly planned lobotomies of prisoners.

11   Ross, Colin A. (2006). The C.I.A. Doctors: human rights violations by American psychiatrists. Richardson, TX: Manitou Communications. See also "Buying a piece of anthropology" (PDF). Wikileaks. Anthropology Today. June 2007; see also "1953: Dr. Wolff and Dr. Hinkle investigate Communist Brainwashing". AHRP. Alliance for Human Research Protection.

Apparently, what the CIA wanted West to deliver for MK-ULTRA was proof that a hypnotic suggestion skillfully implanted could cause a person to do something he wouldn't be aware of or remember – something from which he would be consciously dissociated.

The record contains some suggestion that McVeigh was hypnotized while working at Calspan on the Cornell campus, already having been chosen for participation in a domestic-terror, false-flag attack that would tighten national security laws. His co-workers described him as "distant.".

Considering the hypnosis picture, prominent alumnus West himself, being MK-ULTRA-cleared, could have been the hypnotist of McVeigh – perhaps while at Cornell for a conference or a speaking engagement. Or, any other operative for NE-CIA, perhaps one with a job alongside McVeigh, could have done the deed.

Having actively sought the job just out of the Army, McVeigh left Calspan after only two months and began an itinerant period that lasted two years. He drifted among right-wing groups. All of these were likely infiltrated by federal agents. Then, the run-up to the bombing. The record on McVeigh's behavior during this time suggests strongly that he was in a dissociated state.

Near the Murrah building, in a parking garage, McVeigh removed the Arizona license plate from his planned getaway car. Next, without affixing an Oklahoma plate, he walked away – and thus left his car unready for a getaway.

McVeigh committed the bombing, retrieved the car, drove away, and was arrested 75 minutes later – for no license plate. When asked about this oversight, McVeigh said, "I forgot to put one on."

This was a ludicrously huge "I forgot" to occur in the midst of the most audacious action McVeigh had ever undertaken – a self-declared mission of war. He was a highly trained U.S. soldier and combat veteran, so a fit of nervous amnesia is basically out of the question. The lame excuse of "I forgot" simply cries for an explanation other than normal mental functioning. One good guess is a hypnotic command – for McVeigh to remove one license plate and then "forget" to affix another.

At McVeigh's arrest, by Oklahoma State Trooper Charles Hanger, the record also suggests mental dissociation. According to *Bring the War Home*, by Kathleen Belew,

> When he was arrested, McVeigh had a semiautomatic handgun loaded with a Black Talon "Cop Killer" bullet. The standard pro-

tocol for white-power operatives being pursued was to shoot the police officer and flee.[12]

McVeigh, instead, with a striking lack of emotion, simply said to Hanger, "I'm carrying a concealed weapon." Hanger said this was "odd for a man who'd just bombed 169 people to death."[13]

McVeigh's "unnatural" emotionlessness disturbed the assistant attorney general for Oklahoma's Noble County, Mark Gibson, who said,

> He exuded nothing.... It was like the dutiful soldier – emotions don't come into play, right and wrong don't come into play, what happens next doesn't come into play...[14]

What happened next for McVeigh was months of close monitoring by psychiatrist Jolly West, the hypnotist from CIA's MK-ULTRA mind-control effort. Inmate McVeigh was required to see West 17 times while he was held at El Reno Prison in Oklahoma, a state where West was famous. Why?

The record suggests Dr. Jolly West could guarantee that McVeigh would cover for his handlers. In prison, McVeigh was a captive audience for a skilled hypnotist, and West was an expert. With an ongoing series of hypnotic suggestions – as many as 17 – McVeigh could have been counted on at least not to reveal participation by others in the bombing plan.

And McVeigh's later behavior went beyond just keeping mum – he spoke in vigorous denial of the idea a mastermind had run a bombing plan with himself as a simple functionary. By behaving in a manner protective of his self-image, McVeigh perforce offered further protection to a mastermind or any other conspirators besides himself and Terry Nichols.

McVeigh became fearful, defensive, agitated, argumentative, and challenging when it was suggested that the bombing mastermind was not McVeigh, the trained warrior and strategist, himself alone.

> "Show me where I needed anyone else," McVeigh exclaimed in challenging a *Buffalo News* reporter. "Financing? Logistics? Specialized tech skills? Brainpower? Strategy? Show me where I needed a dark, mysterious 'Mr X'!"[15]

The fact remains that "mysterious" bombs were needed; bombs more sophisticated and powerful than the simple fertilizer bomb in McVeigh's

---

12   Harvard University Press, 2018.
13   *New York Times*, 4/23/95.
14   *Washington Post*, July 12, 1995
15   *The Guardian* June 11, 2001, quoting letter to the *Buffalo News*.

truck – to wreck the Murrah building, burn cars dozens of yards away on Fifth Street, and break windows 16 blocks away – and, to my knowledge, no one has suggested McVeigh planted them.

OKLAHOMA CITY WITNESS ACCOUNTS

A block from the Murrah building, driver Ramona McDonald reported sensing electricity.

> "You could actually hear it," McDonald said. "It made a real loud static electricity sound … like a big swarm of bees."[16]

She also described flashes of blue light – a block away from the bombing site. Inside the Murrah Building's HUD office, which survived the bombing, a victim reported she felt both a static-electricity charge and a heat wave before seeing windows blow in.[17]

ELECTRICITY

Weapons experts are familiar with the electrical effect the witnesses encountered. First observed during the early testing of high-altitude-airburst nuclear weapons, the ElectroMagnetic Pulse (EMP) effect occurs when a rapid acceleration of charged particles causes an intense burst of electromagnetic energy -- in effect, an electromagnetic shock wave.[18]

An EMP device is any weapon, nuclear or conventional, that generates such an electromagnetic shock wave.

HEAT

A "thermo-baric" (heat-pressure) explosive, or fuel-air explosive, can fairly be described as an EMP device that creates a wave full of both heat and shock-level pressure. The witness inside the Murrah building felt both these elements in the bombing. A fuel-air explosive heat/shock wave accounts for cars burned on Fifth Streetdozens of feet away from the building and windows broken up to 16 blocks away.

BLUE FLASHES

The blue flashes described by driver McDonald chime with Michael Riconosciuto's nickname, "Blue Death.", for his advanced thermo-baric bomb.

---

16   Ramona McDonald interview with Jon Roland, Constitition.org Web site. McDonald also described flashes of blue light. Riconosciuto had nicknamed his refined FAE "Blue Death."
17   HUD office, National Public Radio interview, May 23, 1995.
18   "The Electromagnetic Bomb – a Weapon of Electrical Mass Destruction," *Air Power Australia Mirror/US Air Force Air & Space Power Journal Chronicles*, January 27, 2009.

Hercules, Bio-Rad, and Dyno-Nobel

In 1983, CIA agent Earl W. Brian's company Bio-Rad bought the land on which stood the laboratory of Hercules Manufacturing, the Riconosciuto family's well-equipped arms laboratory, formerly a gunpowder factory, in the Bay Area company town of Hercules. This was at the height of Riconosciuto's work as a CIA asset, a time when Brian visited him frequently. Riconosciuto likely developed Blue Death at Hercules Manufacturing while under contract with the Cabazon-Wackenhut arms venture. Brian's Bio-Rad did not acquire the company itself. But two years later, in 1985, a company called Dyno-Nobel acquired the Hercules Manufacturing Company and its lab.

It is likely Dyno-Nobel thus also acquired Riconosciuto's designs for modified FAEs, because by 1990, Dyno-Nobel won a U.S. government contract to deliver a state-of-the-art fuel-air-explosive weapon. Likely from Riconosciuto's design, Dyno-Nobel did deliver to the government a fearsome weapon,[19] which it detonated September 22, 1993, at the US government's Nevada Test Site.[20] To the government, Dyno-Nobel reported the bomb had great destructive power with no radiation, the latter a selling point.[21] A suitcase nuke, with no radiation.

Riconosciuto's Blue Death device was, by 1990, firmly in the hands of the government. In discussing details of the Oklahoma City bombing, Michael Riconosciuto said he recognized the design as his. I hold it as axiomatic that anything available to the CIA is available, perhaps with some effort such as bribery, to NE-CIA as well. And, this crew of Shackleyesque zealots is expert at the kind of threats to firemen that squelched inconvenient reportage on the bombing.

The NE-CIA crew, that prizes above all a rigid national-security state, also benefited greatly from the OKC bombing, following which the U.S. Congress enacted the Anti-terrorism and Effective Death Penalty Act of 1996, with full bipartisan support. The stiff law provides for designation of foreign organizations as terrorist, for tightening of asylum criteria, and "removal or exclusion" from the country of foreigners deemed to be terrorists. In a sense, the Anti-terrorism Act was the initial victory for a renascent political movement, known as American Nativism or less politely as white supremacism that, aided stoutly by post-9/11 spokesmen Rudy Giuliani and James Kallstrom, in 2016 managed to "elect" a U.S. president.

19   Number for the bomb was DAAA-21-90-C-0045, and was manufactured by Dyno-Nobel, Inc., in Salt Lake City. The Department of the Army denies that contract DAAA-21-90-C-0045 exists.
20   US Department of Energy report, "Arms Control and Non-Proliferation Technologies," first quarter 1994.
21   Ibid.

CHAPTER 12

TWA FLIGHT 800, 1996

At the least, this craft did not want to be around when big things were happening; and kept going when the 'sun' came out above it with the documented in-flight explosion.
    – FAA letter to the FBI on FAA radar-tracking of an "unknown surface [craft]" in the area of the TWA Flight 800 explosion

In an air crash that is still controversial,[1] TWA Flight 800 went down off the US coast on July 17, 1996. Two hundred thirty people were killed.

Officials from the National Transportation Safety Board (NTSB) eventually announced that "icing on the wings" caused TWA 800 to crash.

But officials from both the FBI and CIA reportedly had tampered with the evidence available to the NTSB.[2]

This tampering occurred in a probe of the crash led by FBI assistant director in charge James Kallstrom, a probe that the CIA took over, helped by Kallstrom. FBI agents reportedly broke in after-hours to an NTSB-controlled hangar in Calverton, NY, where flight-wreckage evidence was stored.[3] Allegedly, FBI agent Ricky Hahn was observed hammering and flattening pieces of TWA 800 wreckage.[4] To these allegations, Kallstrom merely countered that some FBI agents zealously worked extra hours on the case.

CIA TAMPERING WITH EYEWITNESS ACCOUNTS

After the plane crash, several eyewitnesses including Mike Wire, a bridge worker, told FBI agents he saw a rocket rise and strike TWA 800. As Wire would say years later,

> I saw an object zigzag up off the horizon at about a 40-degree angle, arch over, and culminate in an explosion.[5]

---

1   In mid-2016, for example, author Jack Cashill published his book, *TWA 800: The Crash, the Cover-up, and the Conspiracy*; Regnery History, 2016.
2   Accounts from NTSB investigator Hank Hughes and CIA eyewitness Mike Wire, respectively. in a notarized affidavit attached to a petition by the TWA 800 Project to re-open the investigation.
3   Ibid.
4   Ibid
5   American Thinker website, June 9, 2016.

At the time, the FBI suppressed Wire's account. No straight news release of it ever came. A year later, a "press release" on Wire's account emerged, titled "TWA Flight 800: What Did the Eyewitnesses See?" It was authored by the CIA, an animated video, and it was presented on national television by James Kallstrom of the FBI.

Witness Mike Wire, whom the CIA video called "Eyewitness No. 1," has said the CIA tampered with the testimony he had given to the FBI. Wire recalls,

> I saw nothing of the kind (as presented in the video)... The CIA made a video animation to convince people I was confused. Kallstrom later acknowledged the CIA video was "conjecture, based on a lot of evidence."[6]

And according to journalist Jack Cashill, Kallstrom at one time blurted out that a missile struck TWA 800. Cashill writes,

> TWA attendant Marge Gross, whose brother was killed in the crash, heard a reporter yell to [Kallstrom], "You can't tell me it was anything but a missile that took that plane down." According to Gross, Kallstrom shot back, "You're right, but if you quote me, I'll deny it."[7]

If it was a missile, as Kallstrom blurted out tangentially, whose was it?

THE NAVY MISSILE THEORY

A leading theory is that a mistakenly fired missile from a U.S. Navy submarine hit TWA 800. The Navy was testing missiles in the area at the time of the explosion.[8] However, spokesmen said, the FBI and Pentagon had already investigated the Navy angle, and had been able to dismiss it.

Pentagon spokesman Kenneth Bacon said,

> All missiles owned by the Navy – by any ships, submarines, or planes in the area – have been inventoried, personnel have been interviewed, records have been checked.[9]

---

6   ABC News, July 17, 2000.
7   World Net Daily Web site Nov 12, 2001.
8   This fact emerged in November 1996 after journalist Pierre Salinger said a European intelligence agent told him TWA 800 was shot down by a Navy missile, *New York Times*, November 17, 1996. The "errant-Navy-missile" theory did gain some traction, notably with author Jack Cashill, who wrote two books on the subject and to this day is quoted in Internet accounts. There is some likelihood that Salinger was set up to establish the Navy-missile-accident theory.
9   James Sanders; Jack Cashill, contributor, *First Strike*, Thomas Nelson Inc, 2003.

Kallstrom said, "We know every military asset in the area."[10] FBI No. 2 investigator Lewis Schiliro added, "Based on our investigative efforts, we are confident it was not a military vessel." If not the Navy's missile, then whose?

The record shows one distinct possibility – in a letter to the FBI dated August 21, 1997, a year after the crash, the FAA reports to the FBI that in the explosion area at the time, the FAA radar-tracked an "unknown surface target."[11]

In the letter, an FAA tech said he'd used radar data to determine a "start point" for the vessel's movements. He checked a map to see from which ocean inlet this start point might be. He immediately found something suspect. The FAA radar tech wrote,

> The start position … does not align with any of the inlets providing access … to the ocean.

Huh? Already a sign of subterfuge, and expert subterfuge at that. If the start position for the unknown vessel had been an inlet with access to the ocean, the FAA and FBI could easily have identified it from records kept by harbor-masters on what ships are berthed where. FAA spokewoman Laura Brown said the FAA would not comment on whether the "unknown" craft was ever identified.[12]

This fact fitsa missle-armed helicopter, either pontooned or flying at sea level. The pilot would have been someone able and determined to baffle the FAA, and thus to baffle the FBI; who asked the FAA for help in identifying the craft. Such a person would need to have been in or around federal government, but with a non-government agenda.

The FAA tech concluded that the ambiguous data did clearly show one thing, at least; writing to the FBI,

> At the least, this craft did not want to be around when big things were happening, and kept going when the "sun" came out above it with the documented in-flight explosion.

FAA data shows unambiguously that an unknown surface vessel fled the scene of the TWA 800 explosion. And, the FBI's Schiliro said that vessel, which the bureau was unable to identify, sped away at 30 knots from

10   *Orlando Sentinel*, March 22, 1997.
11   Names were redacted by the FBI. Document posted on Associated Retired Aviation Professionals Web site @"TWA Flight 800 Investigation" (www.100megspopup.com/ark/800BDwbsite-OpngPgAsOf20Apr2001.html)
12   According to Sanders and Cashill, all federal employees are banned from discussing TWA 800.

the TWA 800 crash scene.[13] There's little doubt it's the same mystery vessel, in both the FAA's and the FBI's account. To depart from land and then travel on water, as the FAA said it did, the craft had to have been either a pontoon-fitted plane or a helicopter. And Kallstrom has named the craft fleeing at 30 knots as "a helicopter."

Discussing surface vessels observed in the crash area, Reed Irvine asked Kallstrom,[14]

> Irvine: "What about the one racing out to sea at 30 knots?"
>
> Kallstrom: "That was a helicopter."
>
> Irvine: [clarified] "On the surface [of the water]?"

According to the FBI's Schiliro, the mystery surface vessel was "at least 25-30 feet in length." This is the length of the Boeing 'Little Bird' attack helicopter,[15] which is used primarily by U.S. special-operations forces.[16] Originally a support aircraft, it was eventually retro-fitted to fire missiles.

WHAT MISSILE TYPE?

Early on, within the government, it was suggested that a Stinger (shoulder-fired) missile struck TWA 800.[17] The FBI began covert dredging in the crash area for Stinger missile parts in November 1996. At some point, critics of that idea announced a Stinger couldn't reach an altitude of 13,700 feet – which TWA 800 had reached when it exploded – and the NTSB, too, announced this conclusion in 2000.[18] But that criticism appears to be misinformed or disingenuous.

By early 1996, a modified and more powerful Stinger was available,[19] with an altitude range of 25,000 feet. To make this enhanced Stinger, "Block II," all that was necessary was the retrofitting of an existing Stinger.[20]

---

13   FBI's Lewis Schiliro, speaking in response to questions from a congressional subcommittee, quoted by Jack Cashill, WND Web site, June 21, 2013.

14   Interview of James Kallstrom by Reed Irvine of *Accuracy in Media*, September 14, 1998.

15   Length, 32 feet.

16   Previous to TWA 800's crash, 'Little Bird' attack helicopters were used in U.S. special operations in 1983, 1989, and 1992 (in Grenada, Panama, and Somalia, respectively). David Cenciotti, The Aviationist Web site, May 25, 2011.

17   In August 1997, President Clinton's national coordinator for counterterrorism, Richard Clarke, heard from FBI terrorist expert John O'Neill that FBI eyewitnesses "were pointing to a missile attack, a Stinger." Richard Clarke, Against All Enemies, The Free Press, 2004.

18   "In American History: TWA 800" inamericanhistory.blogspot.com/2012/05/twa-800. html. A June 2000 Washington Post story reported the NTSB had test-fired long-range Stinger anti-aircraft missiles in April 2000.

19   The Stinger, in its early days, was a sort of proprietary weapon for the CIA. *For example, the agency* sent 2,300 *Stinger missiles* to various Mujahideen outfits around 1981.

20   No brand-new missile needed to be produced. Sourced in globalsecurity.org accounts, a Wikipedia article states, "All Air-to-Air Stinger (ATAS) Block II missiles will be modified existing

In the 1980s, the Stinger missile became nearly proprietary to the CIA, when the agency distributed it generously to anti-Soviet Mujahideen fighters in Afghanistan.[21] For its part, the "Little Bird," now an attack heli-copter, capable of firing a Stinger Block II missile, also known as the FIM-92 Stinger,[22] is proprietary to American special-operations units; including the CIA's Special Activities Division. In this scenario, it is perfectly possible, technologically, and even quite plausible, that a modified Stinger missile brought down TWA 800 from the unknown craft cited by FAA and FBI, and that this craft was a pontoon-equipped Little Bird attack helicopter.

Fuel-air Explosive

If it was a missile, what kind of warhead? Witnesses heard and saw two explosions, not one. This is characteristic of a fuel-air weapon and no other.[23]

Jason Fontana, at Westhampton Beach, said, "You heard two big explosions, like two big firecrackers going off."

Fisherman Vic Fehner said, "It started off like a little ball, like a flare. It came down for a few seconds and all of a sudden burst into flames, a big ball of flame."

A Colonel with the New York Air National Guard, who was aloft in a C-130 aircraft, said he saw: "Two large orange fireballs. They looked like comets, coming straight down to the water."[24]

If it was a fuel-air explosion, not too many suspects exist. At the time, somehow, the Russians had the FAE (though their involvement is not at all probable), and former agents around the CIA were able to acquire it,

---

Stinger RMP missiles. The Block II retrofit program will add the Block I modifications plus incorporate a starring IR focal plane array seeker, a new battery, and advanced signal processing capabilities... The seeker permits engagements of helicopters in clutter out to the *8 km* (26,246.7 feet) maximum physical *range* of the missile." In 1996 Raytheon, makers of the Stinger Block I, already had a government contract to retrofit Stinger Block I's into 25,000-foot-range Stinger Block II's.

21   In a rush to ready new U.S. missiles for the First Gulf War, a mysterious, unauthorized test of Stinger missiles was done. According to Defense Department records published by GlobalSecurity.org:

> "The program... did not resemble... soldier training exercises... Most of the firings were... not conducted with soldiers (and) did not contain the conditions under which the Stinger missile is expected to operate."

Who else but the CIA would have run this program?

It is highly likely that the Block II Stinger missile was tested then, too.

22   Wikipedia.

23   The explosion of the missile-carried charge – after a few seconds – ignites any propellant fuel left in the missile. Fuel-air-explosive technology was highly developed by 1996 but its use by Americans was kept secret in the U.S. until after 9/11.

24   William Jasper, *The New American*, October 14, 1996. A second reason to conclude FAE was used is that wreckage was scattered over a remarkably wide range – several miles – despite winds of just 15 knots. Far-flung damage characterizes FAE (see Chapter 10 on the Oklahoma City bombing).

and able if they chose to arm and mount a Little Bird helicopter with pontoons to take off from a land location near New York City, put down in water near the flight path of TWA 800, and fire a Stinger Block II missile to strike TWA 800. Why?

On November 18, 1997, Kallstrom closed the FBI investigation of TWA 800. Twenty-one days later, oddly, he quit the FBI – the agency that had been sworn to diligently investigate domestic-terror attacks as crimes to be tried in a court of law.

Three years later, Kallstrom gained a job in the intelligence community, which was now in charge of investigating domestic-terror attacks in a new way – leaving intelligence operatives, no matter who they were, free from having to testify in U.S. court about their activities.

New York Gov. George Pataki named Kallstrom to head the New York public safety office, a sort of CIA directorship for the State of New York; the kind of role he'd apparently coveted for years.

Based largely on this appointment and his friendship with New York Mayor Rudy Giuliani, in the early 2010s Kallstrom gained a national television presence, delivering polemics for the right wing on Fox television. As of this writing, Kallstrom still holds that role. After the TWA 800 incident, critics suggested President Bill Clinton was covering up a Navy accident. This criticism remains today.

CHAPTER 13

AL QAEDA, ISI, CIA

A l Qaeda ("The Base") could not have arisen as it did around 1988 without earlier U.S. & Saudi arms support for the Mujahideen fighting Soviet invaders in Afghanistan, beginning in 1980, to be distributed by Pakistani Inter-Service Intelligence (ISI) officials. The first of these arms shipments arrived, not from America, but from Egypt. Just months earlier, the weapons had arrived in Cairo under the U.S.-brokered Camp David Accords, having traveled to Egypt via the fraudulent, NE-CIA shipper EATSCO (see Chapter 8). As Egyptian President Anwar Sadat recalled, "The U.S. contacted me, and I gave them the armaments. The transport of arms to the Afghans started from Cairo on U.S. planes."[1]

As we shall see, this Cairo arms cache, tainted by NE-CIA fraud, was the original weaponry equipping the group of Muslim fighters that Osama bin Laden eventually tapped for al Qaeda.

Also coming courtesy of NE-CIA was al Qaeda's basic communications platform.

Reportedly, beginning in 1985, the CIA supplied the mujahideen with "secret communications networks."[2] This was likely the Promis software stolen from Bill and Nancy Hamilton by government officials and then black-marketed, after modification by Michael Riconosciuto, by the CIA's Earl W. Brian – despite theories that bin Laden acquired Promis on the Soviet black market. A simple and popular account has it that double-agent Robert Hanssen stole Promis for the Soviets from the CIA. But according to an American intelligence expert (quoted by the Polish newspaper *Wprost*),

> Yes, it came from the Russians, but not in as big a part as the spook community would have you believe. Nor was it entirely the work of Robert Hanssen. He was merely available to point the finger at.

When Muslim fighters left Afghanistan in 1998, this same "secret communications network" allowed tracking of these valuable human assets

1   Cited in Gabriel Tabarini, *Jihad's New Heartlands*, AuthorHouse, 2011.
2   Phil Gasper, "Afghanistan, CIA, bin Laden, and the Taliban," *International Socialist Review*, November-December 2001.

by both bin Laden and the CIA. These radical Muslims dispersed across dozens of countries.[3] Al Qaeda was an "organization" only through the secret, CIA-provided, communications-and-tracking network.

The CIA's Buzzy Krongard also says al Qaeda was not a unified terrorist group taking orders from bin Laden. Krongard describes bin Laden's role as follows,

> Not a chief executive – more like a venture capitalist. Let's say you and I want to blow up Trafalgar Square. So, we go to bin Laden, and he'll say, "Well, here's some money and some passports, and if you need weapons, see this guy." I don't see him keeping his fingers on everything...[4]

BANKING AND PROMIS

The notorious Pakistani Bank of Credit and Commerce International was an adjunct of the "secret communications network" supplied by the CIA, in that the bank's computers moved the money to supply the mujahideen. BCCI was a money-laundering front for several intelligence agencies, with NE-CIA as an informal partner. Representatives of member spy agencies met at The Safari Club, a Kenyan hunting lodge owned by arms dealer Adnan Khashoggi.

BCCI even had its own "Black Network" of thugs, whose members stole much of the CIA-funded supplies intended for the mujahideen.

The US could distance itself from BCCI after a while, because with the modified Promis software that appeared at the time, NE-CIA could turn any bank it chose into its very own version of BCCI. This was true because many bankers bought bootleg Promis from the CIA's Earl W. Brian and other dealers (at the same time Promis was sold to spy agencies).[5]

Bankers' purchases of modified Promis are important. Legitimate bankers presumably bought it to track details on prospective loan customers, such as previous creditors, addresses, criminal records, employers, and properties.

But into and out of such banks, Michael Riconosciuto's "back-door"-modified Promis allowed NE-CIA to move drug money – payments for arms – without detection. Bill Hamilton, former NSA agent and Promis inventor, told Author Cheri Seymour he believed that,

---

3   In this framework, al Qaeda can be seen as nothing more, or less, than a Western "intelligence asset," as Canadian author Michel Chossudovsky has said.

4   Daily Kos Web site January 20, 2005.

5   David M. Dastych, Canada Free Press, quoting the Polish paper *Wprost*.

Riconosciuto's job was to help (the Contras and the mujahideen) avail themselves of NSA's bank surveillance version of Promis to launder the proceeds from the drug sales.

Riconosciuto, too, has said Promis was used to track details of international drug sales – dealers, shipment dates, contacts – whose profits paid for international arms shipments supplying the Contras and the Mujahideen.

WHO DID ARABS INVOLVED IN 9/11 WORK FOR?

If, as the CIA's Buzzy Krongard observes, Osama bin Laden was more of an investor in al Qaeda than its leader in the field, Arabs involved in 9/11 did not necessarily work for bin Laden. Who else was in a position to locate and hire radicalized Muslims via the "secret communications network" supplied to the mujahideen by the CIA?

That's right, the CIA itself, and its impulsive satellite group, NE-CIA, complicit in the drugs-for-arms deals tracked by Promis. NE-CIA also includes rogues from foreign intelligence agencies. Horst Ehmke, ex-director of the West German secret services, said,

"Terrorists could not have carried out such an operation [as 9/11] without the support of a secret service."[6]

9/11 was planned in Germany, acknowledges Klaus Ulrich Kersten, director of Germany's domestic spy agency, BKA.[7] Going further, author Jeff Pragger's research suggests BKA supported 9/11 financially – with help from Syria's MID (a Safari Club member agency) and Pakistan's ISI.[8]

What, besides money, might American spooks have contributed to 9/11? The clear answer is flight training for the hijackers – or at least a semblance of it for anyone who might be looking. There is a school of thought that attacking planes were remote-controlled, with the "U.S.-flight-trained" Arabs as doomed fall-guys. The standard account is that Mohammed Atta and fellow jihadis hijacked airliners and used them to hit the World Trade Center and the Pentagon.[9]

Atta, and other alleged hijackers, took classes at various U.S. flight schools. But, partly due to poor English skills, they didn't learn enough to have flown Boeing airliners during 9/11.[10] As noted by author Philip Marshall, a former airline pilot,

---

6   *Guardian*, July 21, 2004.
7   *New York Times*, August 24, 2002. Recall that BKA and CIA collaborated in the run-up to Lockerbie (see Chapter 9).
8   WordPress.com Web site, September 2011.
9   Two main alternative theories exist: one, remote-controlled aircraft; and two, planted bombs.
10   "The men couldn't grasp simple radio communications, nor did they possess the mechan-

"The only logical solution is that... by 9/11 ... [somewhere] Arabic-speaking Boeing flight instructors were used."

Wondering where this might have happened, Marshall came to suspect a former CIA airport near Tucson, Arizona. Alleged hijacker Hani Hanjour lived in Tucson. Pinal Airpark is next to Tucson, and during Ted Shackley's Operation Phoenix in Vietnam,[11] supply planes departed from Pinal Airpark. The small airport now houses out-of-service airliners. Marshall wrote of Pinal Airpark,

> I discovered that over 80 perfectly airworthy commercial airliners are scattered around the airport and heavily guarded by a mercenary army with covert Saudi ties.[12] The opportunities are perfect to 'borrow' a Boeing for unlimited and undocumented air training in the dedicated practice range over the desert.[13]

Ostensibly, Pinal County now owns the airport, but visitors are instructed not to photograph any airplanes.[14] Even if the alleged hijackers didn't train at CIA-controlled Pinal Airpark, they *did* train at Huffman Aviation Flight Training in Venice, Florida,[15] which was funded indirectly by NE-CIA, by Kamal Adham, chief of Saudi intelligence and a founder of BCCI, and by Adnan Khashoggi, international arms dealer and owner of the spy-infested Kenyan resort, The Safari Club.

FOREKNOWLEDGE

So far, this fits with an alternate account of 9/11 almost as popular as the standard – that Bush administration officials had warning of an impending attack and chose not to act on it. Much has been written about whether US officials could have prevented 9/11, always with an underlying assumption that foreknowledge necessarily equaled ability to prevent. But no, not necessarily. Why not?

---

ical aptitude for basic flight operations – straight-and-level flight, left and right turns." Kristina Davis, "The San Diego flight instructor who flunked two 9/11 hijackers," San Diego Tribune, Jan 25, 2015.

11   Center for Land Use Interpretation Web site

12   Marshall almost certainly refers to Wackenhut, who contracted for security at a Saudi palace.

13   Marshall, *False Flag 911*, BookSurge *Publishing*, 2008.

14   Marshall, along with his two teenage children and the family dog, either were killed or – as authorities ruled – died in a murder-suicide, in August 2015.

15   As author Jeff Pragger writes, "Atta trained his men and himself at the Huffman Aviation Flight Training school. That school was funded by Wally Hilliard, with Oryx Corporation. Oryx was founded by Adnan Khashoggi and Sheik Kamal Adham, director of Saudi intelligence (1963-79). And during the year before 911, Atta spent time in the company of Mark Schubin and Wolfgang Bhoringer, two CIA pilots... He was a business partner with a CIA recruiter [Hassan Erroudani]... In essence, Mohamed Atta was a US intelligence-community asset working for the United States government." Also cf. E.P. Heidner, former employee of the DIA branch of the Office of Naval Intelligence (ONI), author of "Collateral Damage," COTO Report Web site, September 20, 2012.

Because, *a combination of the world's wealthiest men,* if they had motive for such an atrocity, would have had the power to veto U.S. government prevention of it. One of those men is Adnan Khashoggi. We shall inspect a motive for 9/11 by a peer-group comprising some of the planet's most obscenely wealthy persons.

CHAPTER 14

MASSACHUSETTS – HANSCOM AIR FORCE BASE AND MITRE

Headline 9/11/01: "US Air Defense System fails"
On 9/11, *three separate coincidences coincided at the same time together!* This triple-redundant verbiage may help convey the strangeness, the inherent unacceptability, of what we are asked to believe about 9/11.

> 1. On that terrible Tuesday morning, the "perfect terrorist attack" drafted in 1976 by the U.S. Army (see chapter 2) was carried out – supposedly by a group of Arabs who couldn't have known that such a plan had been drafted, much less its details. Yet details of the attack match perfectly with details of the Army's 1976 draft: airliners crash into the Twin Towers after being hijacked by men armed with box cutters. Obviously, the odds were nearly astronomical against this happening accidently. This enormous unlikelihood must be kept in mind.
>
> 2. Scarcely more credible: Sixty-five years in the making, a state-of-the-art computerized U.S. air defense system malfunctioned on that day and did not block the attack.
>
> 3. Credible – but ominous: On 9/11, former Secretary of the Army Martin R. Hoffman – who in 1976 oversaw the drafting of the perfect terrorist plan – was running Mitretek, a firm virtually identical to its non-profit twin, MITRE, which, as a government contractor, was in control of US air-defense computers at Hanscom Air Force Base.

In what follows, I shall present motive, means, and opportunity for a false-flag attack.

MOTIVE: IN DOING CIA'S ORIGINAL DUTY, THE SERVING OF WALL STREET INTERESTS, TO KEEP OPTION OF "COWBOY" COVERT OPERATIONS

The remarkable and related coincidences detailed above are best understood, I believe, in context of the careers of two men: Martin R. Hoffman and Frank C. Carlucci.

In 1978, secret meetings between Ted Shackley and Frank Carlucci, then Deputy Director of the CIA,[1] contained discussions of a "banana-republic takeover" of the U.S. government (see Introduction).

From that time onward, Carlucci was a protégé of his Princeton chum, Donald Rumsfeld, becoming assistant to Rumsfeld in 1969, directing the Office of Economic Opportunity (OEO); and remaining close as Rumsfeld ascended government ranks. A second Rumsfeld protégé and fellow rising star was Princeton grad Martin R. Hoffman, who enjoyed being "alter ego" to Secretary of Defense James R. Schlesinger between 1973 and 1975 – beginning at a time when Schlesinger had just left his post as Deputy Director of the CIA.

During that time, on December 22, 1974, reporter Seymour Hersh broke the story of the CIA "family jewels," an amalgam of super-secret and illegal covert operations – including the planning, which Carlucci reportedly participated in, of the murder of Congolese Prime Minister Patrice Lumumba.[2]

In the uproar that followed, it became clear that Congress would investigate the CIA about Hersh's revelations. So, emergency meetings were soon held on how the CIA might weather the coming probe. Present were officials from the Defense Department, the CIA, and the State Department. The first such meeting came on January 4, 1975, at which Secretary of State Henry Kissinger warned that the CIA could lose its ability to do covert foreign operations. He said, "You will end up with a CIA that does only reporting, not operations."

On February 20, 1975, at a second emergency meeting, alongside Kissinger those present included Defense Department legal counsel Martin R. Hoffman, Defense Secretary James Schlesinger, and White House Chief of Staff Donald Rumsfeld. Absent was CIA Director William Colby. The pressing topic was "how much to reveal" to a Congressional committee.[3] The question arose of whether committee members would leak, to Congress as a whole and thus, possibly, to the public, what the CIA turned over. As a transcript of the meeting reveals, Hoffman and Kissinger believed the needed response was to stonewall.

Emphasizing "security" – i.e., keeping secrecy – Hoffman said, "But don't we have to preserve their [committee members'] ability to keep security?"[4]

---

1   Probably, after serving as Secretary of Defense between 1987 and 1989, Carlucci was on the Wackenhut board of directors.
2   Carlucci has denied this.
3   Gerald R. Ford Library, photocopy "Memorandum of Conversation involving Kissinger," archive.org.
4   Ibid.

Hoffman essentially equated U.S. capabilities in national defense with a CIA completely free from scrutiny. Why? Apparently, Hoffman was heeding Kissinger's fearful warning.

It is likely those present resented Congress investigating the CIA – and harbored thoughts of revenge. At the time, with Jimmy Carter campaigning strongly for president, perceived by the right as certain to further Congressional pressure on the CIA, thoughts of revenge must have been beginning, too, for CIA agent Ted Shackley, former CIA Deputy Director Vernon Walters, and future CIA Deputy Director Frank Carlucci (even though Carlucci was abroad, as ambassador to Portugal).

And so it happened that barely five months later, on August 5, 1975, Hoffman was appointed Secretary of the Army. Three months after that, Rumsfeld was appointed Secretary of Defense.

It is hard not to see connections among the following four closely spaced historical events:

1. The 1975 CIA-revelations meeting including Hoffman and Kissinger;

2. the 1975 job promotions of Hoffman and Rumsfeld;

3. the 1976 U.S. Army draft, under Hoffman, of "the perfect terrorist attack" on the Twin Towers; and

4. The 1978 secret meetings of Shackley, Carlucci, and Walters in McLean, Virginia to discuss a "banana-republic" takeover.

MEANS: ASSEMBLING TOOLS FOR A FALSE-FLAG ATTACK
UNLIMITED MONEY:

During this period, the record also shows that NE-CIA was raising black money, lots of it. This money was looted from the nation's banks and savings-and-loans, in an activity that apparently began with Texas banks – becoming known as the Texas Rent-A-Bank scandal – and expanded notoriously to include savings-and-loans across the country.[5]

In this massive theft, financial institutions issued billions of dollars in loans that were never repaid, with most of the bad-loan money disappearing, before much of it was eventually traced to the funding of CIA covert operations, including the Nicaraguan Contra army. Men like real estate tycoon and convicted felon, G. Wayne Reeder, were reportedly culpable in this.[6]

---

5   Steve Pizzo et al, *Inside Job: The Looting of America's Savings and Loans*, McGraw Hill, 1989.
6   Ibid.

Reeder, we recall, escorted the CIA's Earl W. Brian to the arms demonstration in 1981, attended by two Contra generals and sponsored by Cabazon-Wackenhut joint arms venture (see Chapter 1).[7] Wackenhut's board of directors reportedly has included Frank Carlucci.[8] And, during the years from 1975 to around 1988, money looted from the nation's S&Ls was being amassed for covert operations by NE-CIA. It is estimated that a false-flag attack on the Twin Towers would have cost billions of dollars.

INTEROPERABILITY

After nearly 20 years' worth of black money had been amassed by 1988, seven years later, in 1995, Martin R. Hoffman gained control of another asset apparently necessary to the uber-villains behind 9/11: interoperability of the nation's defense computers. Hoffman gained this control through his chairmanship at Mitretek, private twin to MITRE, the non-profit that, under government contract, *researched interoperability among national-defense computers.*[9] The record suggests that at some point, somehow, whoever the perpetrators were, they obtained interoperability-control of the nation's defense computers, and that they had this control on 9/11.

Who had both multiple motives and multiple opportunities to ask Hoffman for such a favor? NE-CIA did. The motives were fervent desires to take revenge against Congress and Jimmy Carter and to free American agents to topple foreign governments in favor of wealthy U.S. investors.[10] Among zealous spies, these motives had grown naturally out of the fear of Soviet communism that permeated America after World War II.

OPPORTUNITY: HANSCOM AIR FORCE BASE, FAA CENTER, 9/11/01

With the goal of preventing a Soviet air attack, MITRE, a newly formed non-profit, went to work in 1957 to computerize and centralize the nation's air-defense system – NORAD. MITRE is a government-funded

---

7   Martha Honey, *Hostile Acts*, University Press of Florida, 1994.

8   At the time of the 1978 Shackley-Carlucci-Walters meetings, a like-minded Martin R. Hoffman worked 10 miles away, running a Washington, DC law office. There's little doubt Hoffman would have been welcome at those Shackley-Carlucci-Walters meetings and little doubt that in ensuing years these four government insiders kept some contact. In May 1988, for example, Defense Secretary Carlucci named Hoffman to a new commission on closing unneeded military bases.

9   Indira Singh, herself previously a Defense Department contractor, pointed to MITRE's role at the FAA while testifying at the 9/11 Citizens' Commission hearings in New York City, September 2004.

10   A third and related reason for NE-CIA in the late 1990s to have sought interoperability of the nation's defense computers was that several years previous, federal investigators began probes into massive money laundering by U.S. banks, likely building on evidence gained in an earlier probe of American S&Ls, where massive looting through bad loans was found and eventually linked to CIA funding of the Contras (such 1990s money-laundering operations are discussed in the next chapter).

spinoff from Massachusetts Institute of Technology (MIT). By the mid-1990s, MITRE had a for-profit twin, Mitretek, separate from MITRE only on paper.[11] Chairman of the board of directors at Mitretek was Martin R. Hoffman – former Defense Department counsel (while Congress was moving to investigate the CIA) and former Secretary of the Army (while the Army drafted "the perfect terrorist attack" mimicked on 9/11).

So, what? For years, MITRE had been researching "interoperability" of the nation's defense computers – how a person controlling an FAA computer, say, could instantly access a NORAD computer's database – according to former Defense Department contractor Indira Singh, who told the 9/11 Commission, on September 9, 2004,

> In the basement of the FAA (at Hanscom AFB) for two years prior to 9/11 (MITRE's) specific job was to look at interoperability issues the FAA had with NORAD and the Air Force in the case of an emergency.

Singh said that another company, Ptech, also worked in the FAA basement. She continued,

> If anyone was in a position to know that… there was a *window of opportunity to insert software or to change anything–* it would have been Ptech along with MITRE.

Ptech was investigated by the government for complicity in 9/11 but was cleared. As far as I have been able to determine, no investigation of MITRE was ever conducted. Accounting at least partially for this could be MITRE's long-standing Defense Department connection to MIT[12] and its connection to career government-insider Martin Hoffman.

Prior to 9/11, it is likely that MITRE had "discovered" on its own or been informed by NE-CIA that interoperability for computers – in the sense of an ability to access from outside a database coded in a computer language unique to that database – was technologically available. It was simply a matter of installing a "back door" capability, as the Promis software possessed after it was modified by Michael Riconosciuto (at the CIA's behest, in the Wackenhut/Cabazon joint venture).

---

11   Evidently, spinoff Mitretek exists only to give legal cover to ongoing for-profit work that, allegedly improperly, MITRE had been doing previously. "The new ballgame is to develop a credible private sector entity," said Barry Horowitz, Mitretek president/CEO and former MITRE president/CEO. Washington Post, February 23, 1996.

12   Redmond, K. et al, "From Whirlwind to MITRE: The R&D Story of The SAGE Air Defense Computer," Cambridge, Massachusetts: Massachusetts Institute of Technology.

Said Indira Singh, "The (FAA) software was very like Promis.[13]

The FAA software could easily have been fitted with "back-door" interoperability – of a kind that would give an outsider not only readability access to its database but also executive-operator control, the kind that could shut down particular operations of the FAA computers, such as recording the arrival of unknown aircraft, and could do this in a way undetectable to FAA operators.[14] There is evidence that MITRE-controlled FAA computers were "down" temporarily on 9/11. Spokeswoman for MITRE Jennifer Shearman has said she is unable to say why the Promis-like MITRE technology apparently failed on 9/11.[15]

After 9/11, loathe to risk revealing defense procedures, Pentagon generals told partial truths to the 9/11 Commission about what happened. This got so bad that, as the *Washington Post* reported,[16]

> Suspicion of wrongdoing [lying to investigators] ran so deep that the 10-member commission, in a secret meeting at the end of its tenure in summer 2004, debated referring the matter to the Justice Department for criminal investigation, according to several commission sources.

Specifically, the generals tended to deny that simple RADAR detection of incoming mystery aircraft could automatically launch U.S. defense jets.

> [FAA air traffic controllers] "had to pick up the phone and literally dial us," said Maj. Douglas Martin, public affairs officer for NORAD, Boston Center.

It is likely that the FAA call to NORAD came from Hanscom Air Force Base near Boston. NORAD's Major Martin clearly implies that given the ineffectiveness of defense response, the FAA call to NORAD came too late.

Also, after 9/11, with his friend Donald Rumsfeld again Defense Secretary, Martin Hoffman was made Rumsfeld's assistant in prosecuting a new U.S. war, in Afghanistan.[17]

In conclusion, the record suggests that the perfect terrorist plan was drafted by Hoffman's Army team at the behest of NE-CIA in the persons

---

13   In an interview with author Michael Ruppert.

14   This is the kind of interoperability that the CIA has long coveted and that it achieved with the bootleg sales of modified Promis to foreign spy agencies and to banks. This coveted capability finally made the news in 2010, when it was revealed that the CIA and the Mossad had teamed up to disrupt Iranian nuclear computers with a planted malware called Stuxnet.

15   Christopher Bollyn, published on American Free Press Web site, April 1, 2005

16   August 3, 2006.

17   Newsletter, Association of the United States Army, September 1, 2014.

of, among others, Ted Shackley, Frank Carlucci, and Vernon Walters, the guys on the park bench in McLean, Virginia – toward such a day when NE-CIA, in its evolving membership, might find it necessary to implement the attack plan. The blueprint was on the shelf for 25 years, primed and ready. At the least, such a scheme would have been impossible to forget, and if the "right" circumstances were ever to arise, its diabolical beauty would have made the temptation to use it amplify irresistibly.

As it turns out, that "right" moment did arise: in the late 1990s, a years-long probe of black-market money laundering was near to exposing a long-standing connection of U.S. covert operations to international drugs-for-arms deals, and thus to the intimate involvement of Wall Street wheeler-dealers in this criminal economy.

In the next chapter, we will review how an impending crisis for Wall Street and its clients, the self-styled "Masters of the Universe", appears to have motivated 9/11.

CHAPTER 15

THE WASHING MACHINE

NEW YORK CITY AND BALTIMORE: DEUTSCHE BANK

At time of this writing, numerous reports have exposed money-laundering at Deutsche Bank, which has operated in the U.S. since 1872 – some of this laundering alledgly involving the current occupier of the White House. Twenty years ago, the reports weren't there, but the money-laundering machine sure was. From 1995 to 1998, the bank employed a notorious, eventually convicted money-launderer, Kevin Ingram, to do "special" transactions exclusively for "High-Net-Worth Individuals," with no deal worth less than $1 million and many worth several billions of dollars. On June 12, 2001, three months before 9/11, Ingram was arrested on suspicion of money laundering to aid an international arms-for-heroin scheme.

The same day, an ocean away, French police arrested two of the world's wealthiest men, also on suspicion of money laundering – Henri de Castries and Claude Bebear, members of the secretive Bilderberg Group.[1] With these three high-profile arrests coming on the same day, the record suggests international authorities were closing in on a world-wide arms-to-heroin money-laundering ring involving the super-wealthy, with Deutsche Bank neck-deep in the conspiracy.

However, three days later, on June 15, 2001, the U.S. Office of Inspector General had opened an investigation into allegations that "[Securities Exchange Commission] Enforcement has improperly destroyed records relating to Matters Under Inquiry ("MUIs") over the past two decades.[2] This was ominous because SEC Enforcement is a very early link in the chain of U.S. agencies fielding allegations of money laundering. And, as we shall see, SEC destruction of records figured large in the aftermath of 9/11.

---

1   The Bilderberg Group, comprising bankers, corporate presidents, and the like, is a long-standing international group that makes no secret of its general goal of keeping the world running in what it considers an orderly manner. Its specific doings are rigorously secret, a secrecy generously maintained by the mainstream press, for which complicity. David Rockefeller thanked the corporate press in 1991, saying, "It would have been impossible for us to develop our plan for the world if we had been subjected to the lights of publicity."

2   Office of Inspector General report, October 5, 2011.

The Run-up to 9/11

In 1991, a world-wide investigation began into money-laundering practiced by arms-for-drugs dealers and cooperative intelligence agents. That year, former CIA operative Buzzy Krongard had become chief executive officer at the Alex Brown & Sons bank in New York City. In early 1994, New York State auditors discovered something strange at Bankers Trust Corporation.[3] Millions of dollars in unclaimed customer funds had disappeared. In 1997, steered by Krongard, Bankers Trust acquired Alex Brown & Sons.Just months later, in February 1998, Krongard abruptly returned to the CIA – becoming counselor to the director of the agency.

At that point, in stepped Deutsche Bank, which acquired Bankers Trust/Alex Brown assets, in 1999, becoming Deutsche Bank AB.

Deutsche Bank and Money-laundering by Extremely Wealthy Men

The notorious arms dealer Adnan Khashoggi, whose peak worth was around $4 billion, dealt at Deutsche Bank AB with Buzzy Krongard's protégé Mayo Shattuck III, who resigned abruptly after 9/11.[4] According to a study by Brown University, Khashoggi was likely the go-between for NE-CIA's putative founder Ted Shackley and the head of the Shah of Iran's secret police.[5] In Khashoggi's world, it is routine that heroin is used to pay for arms.

At the time of his arrest on June 12, 2001, Kevin Ingram had left Deutsche Bank. The specific nefarious deal was for Stinger missiles to Pakistan. Just 13 days before 9/11, Ingram pled guilty, agreeing to testify against co-defendants. If there was ever a time when the world's wealthiest men were interested in having money-laundering records destroyed, this was it.

The record suggests that 9/11, among other purposes, was a tool used to destroy computerized reports from money-laundering probes.[6] It suggests further that investigative reports would have linked wealthy depositors at Deutsche Bank with depositors at a particular French bank that was connected not only to the team of de Castries and Bebear but also, historically, to the CIA.

---

3   *New York Times, May 30, 1999.* It was eventually found that bankers at BTC had improperly listed this money as assets.

4   Mark Gaffney, *Black 9/11*, Trine Day, 2016. US Sen. Carl Levin claimed that Deutsche Bank AB was one of 20 prominent U.S. banks associated with money laundering.

5   *"Understanding the Iran-Contra Affair,"* https://www.brown.edu/Research

6   9/11, in its complexity, obviously took years to plan, but plans typically are shelved for an appropriate moment at which point a "go" signal is given. Operatives are assembled in the interim.

THE FRENCH CONNECTION: BANQUE WORMS

De Castries and Bebear ran AXA, a large insurance company. At the time French police arrested the two Bilderbergers, U.S. media reports said the focus of investigation was AXA subsidiary PanEuroLife. The reports did not mention the apparently more important role of a second AXA subsidiary, Banque Worms.[7] Police suspected "funds of criminal origin" deposited at Banque Worms to be the first element in the money-laundering scheme allegedly involving de Castries and Bebear.[8]

The history of Banque Worms bears out the suspicion held by French police. The bank has always attracted types of people interested in keeping secret the affairs of the very wealthy. As journalist Tony Papert notes, during World War II Banque Worms was a "cutout," a vehicle through which top financier families could deploy the means to keep their wealth – no matter what happened to the French government or the great majority of France's citizens.[9]

At least as early as 1980, Banque Worms became a cutout for the CIA's cowboy wing of agents and ex-agents led by Ted Shackley. After being fired by President Jimmy Carter in 1979 Shackley vowed to continue the cowboys' anti-communist mission.

The 1980 election pitted anti-communist bulldog Ronald Reagan against incumbent Carter. At the time, Israel was selling arms to Iran for use against their common enemy – Saddam Hussein's Iraq. Iran was paying Israel for these weapons out of its oil profits. At the same time, Carter was negotiating with Iran for release of 52 American hostages held by Iran.[10]

Stepping into this scenario, Ronald Reagan backers opened their own negotiations, secret and unofficial, with Iran. Reagan campaign chairman and soon-to-be CIA director William Casey offered[11] that the U.S. (CIA) would take over payments for arms shipped to Iran by Israel if, in exchange, Iran would delay the release of American hostages until after the 1980 election. For the "drop" of CIA secret payments to Israel on behalf of Iran, a Banque Worms account should be used.[12] Iran agreed.

7   BBC, June 13, 2001.

8   "Affaire de Blanchiement," pyxel.info Web site, June 14, 2001. *L'Express* mentioned only a single individual, a French gangster, as being of interest to investigators. L'Express August 30, 2001.

9   *Executive Intelligence Review*, January 6, 2006. Papert is describing the Synarchist movement, a precursor of the modern Bilderberg Group.

10   Between 1980 and 1988, Iran intermittently took U.S. hostages. Out of this situation grew a long period of illegal and secret arms deliveries to Iran by the U.S. spook community, in exchange for hostage release.

11   *Counterpunch* July 11, 2014. The report by Carmelo Ruiz-Marrero attributes its substance to Gary Sick, *October Surprise: America's Hostages in Iran and the Election of Ronald Reagan*, Crown, 1991; and to former Iranian president Abolhassan Bani-Sadr, *My Turn to Speak: Iran, the Revolution and Secret Deals With the US*, Potomac Publishing, 1991.

12   Former Israeli agent Ari Ben Menashe, *Profits of War*, Sheridan Square Publishing, 1992.

Arranged by Reagan campaign director William Casey (soon appointed CIA director), an Israeli agent dropped drug profits from Central America generated by NE-CIA into an Israeli-controlled account at Banque Worms, Geneva, from which money could be withdrawn by the Israeli company supplying Iran with military equipment.[13] More of such funds went into an account controlled by the CIA's Earl W. Brian in Phoenix, Arizona. William Casey and Earl W. Brian were involved at the time with the Wackenhut-Cabazon joint arms venture (see Chapter 1).

Keeping its part of the deal, Iran delayed the release of its hostages until January 20, 1981 – the day Ronald Reagan was inaugurated as President.

This affair was dubbed, the "October Surprise." Subsequent arms-for-hostages exchanges with Iran that ran through 1987 became the "Iran-Contra Scandal." NE-CIA, in the persons of Lt. Col. Oliver North, and arms dealer and Bilderberger Adnan Khashoggi, was involved in both segments of the deals.Not too long after Iran-Contra was exposed, De Castries' and Bebear's AXA entered the picture – to acquire the Banque Worms assets, in 1996. Then, French police began looking into money-laundering at Banque Worms, in the investigation that led to the arrests of de Castries and Bebear. Previously, in June 2011, de Castries and Bebear's AXA had sold Banque Worms to Deutsche Bank. This sale came in October 2000, at a time when AXA was insurer for Deutsche Bank properties in the Manhattan (ground zero) area.

This transaction suggests that assets deposited at the de Castries/Bebear- and CIA-connected Banque Worms were intermingled with assets deposited at the Kevin Ingram-Buzzy Krongard-CIA-connected Deutsche Bank. These "funds of criminal origin" belonging to some of the world's wealthiest men later were acquired as assets by a division of Hong Kong & Shanghai Bank, an institution often penalized for failing to prevent money laundering. As such, the public record is full of facts suggesting that just previous to 9/11, significant evidence was in hand and significant arrests and prosecutions were imminent among the planet's super-wealthy and their cooperative intelligence agents on charges of arms-to-heroin money laundering.

But, no significant prosecutions and prison sentences came, outside of Kevin Ingram's, from the decade-long investigations. De Castries and Bebear were never formally charged, much less imprisoned. Khashoggi

---

13 Ibid.

was never arrested. Why not? An extremely likely explanation is, "the evidence was destroyed."

After the June 12, 2001 grillings of Kevin Ingram, Henri de Castries, and Claude Bebear by investigators, a supremely compelling motive existed for their cooperative intelligence agents – NE-CIA, perhaps meeting at the Safari Club resort owned by Adnan Khashoggi – to push the button on a plan already in place, funded, and staffed with operatives, including some Muslims; namely, a plan *to destroy computerized money-laundering investigative records dangerous to NE -CIA by means of a false-flag attack on the World Trade Center, where countless such records were stored – an attack using airliners hijacked by foreign "terrorists" carrying box-cutters* (the plan drawn up in 1976 by the US Army, see Chapter 2 and 14).[14]

RECORDS DESTROYED

During the 1990s, the building called World Trade Center 6 was home base to the El Dorado Task Force money-laundering investigation. Some 55 agencies, federal and state, worked to compile records. These computerized records were destroyed in the 9/11 attack and the 55 money-laundering investigations were shut down.[15]

After 9/11, computer-data-retrieval experts were hired, and they recovered some data from World Trade Center computers. According to reports obtained by journalist Michael Ruppert, data recovered showed that more than $100 million in illegal money transactions rushed through World Trade Center computers before and during the 9/11 attack.

A Deutsche Bank employee phoned him, Ruppert writes, to say that five minutes before the Twin Towers attack, Deutsche Bank's computer system was "

> ... seized by an outside, unknown entity [and] every file swiftly uploaded to an unidentified locality."[16]

The record suggests it's likely that back-door Promis software was used to make this reported seizure of Deutsche Bank's Trade Center computer system. It is quite possible that in addition to destruction by fire, many computerized money-laundering records were destroyed on 9/11 by Promis-assisted invasions of computers at the World Trade Center.

14   A plan able to use Muslim operatives from the network cultivated by the CIA to fight Soviets in Afghanistan (see Chapter 13).
15   Each agency was redirected, "to investigate terrorist financing."
16   Ruppert, *Crossing the Rubicon*, New Society Publishers, Canada, 2004, pp. 243-247. This type of operation appears to have been repeated in 2016 with the theft of emails from the Democratic National Committee office.

FOREKNOWLEDGE AND RESPONSIBILITY

So far, we have discussed destruction of records that chronicled arms-to-heroin money laundering. But in the saga of 9/11, even more important evidence was destroyed. Also destroyed were documents that identified persons with apparent foreknowledge of, and responsibility for, the destruction of the towers; documents that would, in the legal sense, have identified a particular institutional investor, a customer of Deutsche Bank, who was an accomplice-before-the-fact of the crime.

EARLY SEPTEMBER 2001 – THE DEUTSCHE BANK-BROKERED "PUT" OPTIONS ON UNITED AIRLINES STOCK

Some of the planes used in the attack belonged to United Airlines. On the Chicago Stock Exchange, normally the number of "put-option" trades on United Airlines stock – amounting to bets that the stock would fall – ran around 400 per day. On September 6, 2001, however, this number was 4,744.[17] After 9/11, United Airlines stock crashed and all buyers of the 4,744 options profited. Startlingly, 9/11 Commission records reveal a single buyer took all but a few of the 4,744 put options on United Airlines stock on September 6, 2001. This is a strong indication of foreknowledge of the attack to come, though investigators found it was all just a coincidence.

THE 9/11 COMMISSION REPORT: FOOTNOTE 30 TO CHAPTER 5.

In its footnote 30 to Chapter 5, the report said,

> A single U.S.-based institutional investor... purchased 95 percent of the United Airlines put (options) on September 6, 2001.[18]

THE SEC IS SUSPECT

In making this finding the investigators used documents supplied by the Securities Exchange Commission. David Callahan,[19] in a FOIA request, asked for those records concerning the "single investor" who bought 95 percent of the United Airlines put options on September 6, 2001. Startlingly, the SEC wrote to Callahan,

> In response to your request seeking copies of the documentary evidence referred to in footnote 30 of Chapter 5 of the ... (9/11)

---

17   "September 11 Put Call," Snopes.com Web site.
18   September 11 Commission Report, Chapter 5, footnote 130.
19   Executive editor of SmartCEO.

Commission Report, we have been advised that the potentially responsive records have been destroyed.[20]

Office of Inspector General watchdogs investigated whether these important records had been destroyed illegally (OIG Case 567), but SEC spokesman Raphael Kozolchyk dodged the question,[21] saying first he was too busy to inquire, then, "I don't have access to that report," and finally became unresponsive when asked why not.

The options buyer avoided the risk that he might be identified while claiming his options profit. He never claimed the money, reported as $5 million. On September 29, 2001, the *San Francisco Chronicle* wrote, "This smells real bad." But evidence is available concerning the milieu in which the options buyer lived – the crowd he ran with. It is the same crowd we have been discussing in this chapter – the Deutsch Bank-Banque Worms-CIA crowd.

The large clutch of United Airlines put options was bought through Deutsche Bank-Alex Brown, at its Baltimore office, according to researcher Lars Schall.[22] Max Keiser, a former options trader with experience at Alex Brown & Sons, told Schall,

> There are many aspects concerning these (put-)option purchases that have not been disclosed yet. ... When the attacks occurred, ABS was owned by Deutsche Bank. An important person at ABS was Buzzy Krongard. I have met him several times at the offices in Baltimore.
>
> Krongard had transferred (at the time of the 911 attacks) to become executive director at the CIA [a promotion from Krongard's previous CIA job as counselor to the agency director]. The option purchases in which ABS was involved occurred in the offices of ABS in Baltimore. The 'noise' which occurred between Baltimore, New York, and Langley (CIA headquarters) was interesting, as you can imagine, to say the least.[23]

---

20   SEC response to a Freedom of Information Act request by David Callahan. as reported by Mark Gaffney, May 25, 2016, at "Information Clearing House" Web site.

21   Certainly as a practical matter, specific records that could indicate foreknowledge of 9/11 are, arguably, too important to the national interest to be destroyed under a general policy established for reasons that were, as is clear from SEC discussion of the matter, bureaucratic in nature and had nothing to do with the national interest. The following is from an October 5, 2011 OIG report: "On June 15, 2011, Office of Inspector General opened an investigation into allegations... that Enforcement has improperly destroyed records relating to Matters Under Inquiry ("MUIs") over the past two decades, and that... concerning the SEC's potential unauthorized destruction of MUI records, the SEC made misleading statements in... response to (a query from) the National Archives and Records Administration."

22   Lars Schall, "Insider Trading on 9/11," *Asia Times*, March 21, 2012, and Global Research, September 17, 2015.

23   Ibid.

Likely as a means to quiet this noise, Deutsche Bank quickly hired away the top money-laundering investigator at the SEC, Richard Walker. As we have seen, NE-CIA had compelling motive and ample means to mount a false-flag attack. And, as one of the most powerful cabals in the world, it had nothing but opportunity when push finally came to shove, as the record indicates it did with the imediate wrapping-up, following 9/11, of the international money-laundering investigation pursuing final leads gained in the interrogations on June 12, 2001 of Kevin Ingram, Henri de Castries, and Claude Bebear.

Additionally, 9/11 stampeded the U.S. Congress into passing over-whelmingly the oppressive USA Patriot Act, and an equally cowed American public cheered this legislation.

CHAPTER 16

ANTHRAX

S hortly after September 11, mailed envelopes containing anthrax were opened in the eastern United States. Some people opening them died. Others fell ill. These anthrax mailings, widely publicized, added to the terror Americans felt after the destruction of the Twin Towers and the attack on the Pentagon.

Suspected first were "Arab terrorists." Suspected next were "disgruntled Americans" with access to anthrax. These Americans included Steven Hatfill and Bruce Ivins, who worked on anthrax vaccine at the U.S. Army's Fort Detrick, Maryland. Ivins died not long after being announced as a suspect. With that, the FBI closed the case, naming Ivins the culprit. Prominent legislators and their staffs had been targeted.

As of 1952, the CIA ran a military-offensive biowarfare research program at Fort Detrick,[1] and after that, the agency never really left. In 2001, CIA agent Earl W. Brian's company, Hadron Advanced Biosystems, held an anthrax-research contract at Fort Detrick – despite Brian's being in jail at the time for financial fraud. Brian's partner and front man, Soviet defector Kanatjan Alibekov, ran the Hadron venture at Fort Detrick.

Some speculation arose that Alebikov was the anthrax mailer. No evidence or motive suggests this, but much evidence suggests the mailer knew Alebikov and had access to anthrax through him. In 1991, the USSR fell while anthrax expert Alebikov was in the U.S., inspecting American bioweapons facilities. On this tour, Alebikov met the top figures in the Fort Detrick anthrax-research program, including Charles Bailey and William C. Patrick III.[2] He defected to the U.S. in 1992. Bailey and Patrick debriefed him and conferred frequently with Alibekov over the next year.[3] Next, Bailey hired Alebikov onto Fort Detrick's anthrax-research program.

---

1   20 MAY 1975 MEMORANDUM FOR: Director of Central Intelligence SUBJECT: CIA Activities at Fort Detrick, Maryland.

2   "Alibek defected to America in October 1992 and spent much of the next year being debriefed by CIA officers." BBC History, February 17, 2017, "Silent Weapon: Smallpox and Biological Warfare".

3   Bob Coen, Eric Nadler, "Dead Silence: Fear and Terror on the Anthrax Trail," *Counterpoint* 2009 - Political Science?

Soon, the clever idea of *mailing* deadly anthrax arose in discussions between William C. Patrick and the CIA. Patrick was hired,[4] and in turn hired Alebikov and Hadron to help predict the dispersal and damage capability of mailing "weaponized" anthrax.[5]

In May 2000, Hadron received a defense contract from DARPA.[6] Presumably, the contract called for vaccine research. Alebikov's name was now Ken Alibek.

In March, 2001, Alibek applied to patent a method of weaponizing anthrax by encapsulating spores in silica, to make them more inhalable. He had a standout formula. Stanford University professor Steven Block has concluded that the anthrax-mail attacker used a powder made with "the so-called optimal U.S. recipe" for weaponized anthrax. At a conference of the American Physical Society, Block said,

"That means they either had to have information from the United States or maybe they *were* the United States."[7] (Author's italics)

Investigators turned up little. The *New York Times* commented on this, writing,

> [The FBI] may be standing back because the person... involved... may have secret information that the United States government would not like to have divulged.[8]

This was a veiled reference to Alibek. But the record suggests it was Alibek's spy friends, not he, who deserved scrutiny. Defector Alibek owed a debt to friends in NE-CIA, such as Hadron founder, agent Earl W. Brian, who was the first to give Alibek a job. When and if he was approached for a favor, ("Ken, for national-security purposes, give me some of your weaponized anthrax.") Alibek would have been in no position to refuse.

The anthrax-mailings, were a follow-up to 9/11. As we have seen, there was plenty of opportunity for NE-CIA to launch a weaponized-anthrax attack, and such an attack would have been regarded as useful as an enhancement to the terror, scaring Americans so much that Congress would pass the sweeping and arguably repressive Patriot Act.

---

4   Patrick was commissioned by SAIC, the No. 1 holder of government contracts – and well-known as the primary private resource for the CIA, in conjunction with Battelle Memorial Institute, a non-profit.

5   Leonard G. Horowitz, Tetrahedron Journal, August, 30, 2002. The project resembles the Army's 1976 draft of an airplane attack on the World Trade Center. Kenneth J. Dillon, "Was Abderraouf Jdey the Anthrax Mailer?" Scientia Press Web site, undated.

6   OTC Bulletin Board

7   *Dallas Morning News*, April 4, 2002

8   William Broad, *New York Times*, Dec. 13, 2001

Alibek himself has suggested the anthrax mailer might be a government contractor; an "astounding" claim, one reporter said; but not far-fetched in context of the covert world sketched out here and in the work of many other concerned Americans.

The FBI then dropped the investigation into Ken Alibek's hands – "because no one in the world has made more weapons-grade anthrax than he has." After that, nothing conclusive ever came from Mr. Alibek, or any other investigation into the dramatic encore of the 9/11 attacks. It was a clean getaway.

CHAPTER 17

AGAINST THE CLINTONS

This chapter is about how Americans lost the ability to acquire truth. After 9/11, a battle was fought, and lost, over Americans' right to truth. This loss was gradual, beginning long before the "alternative facts" and "fake news" notions that came current in the 2016 election. These notions were just signs that this quiet war was over.

A battle against the Clintons, Bill and Hillary, succeeded in dissociating from truth two ideas historically linked to truth: virtue and character. On May 23, 1993, Michael Kelly was still regarded as a legitimate journalist[1] when he wrote a "character piece" for the *New York Times* on Hillary Clinton, called "Saint Hillary." Kelly's somewhat odd piece suggested that Mrs. Clinton is a person who claims to have virtue, and that by extension, her husband Bill also claims to have virtue.[2]

Kelly characterized First Lady Clinton as a crusader who wanted to capitalize on preaching "the politics of virtue." But, Kelly wrote,

> The true nature of her politics makes the ambition of Hillary Rodham Clinton much larger than merely personal. She clearly wants power, and has already amassed more of it than any First Lady since Eleanor Roosevelt. But that ambition is merely a subcategory of the infinitely larger scope of her desires.[3]

Seven months later, in January 1994, the "Troopergate" story concerning Bill Clinton eased surreptitiously from tabloid into mainstream publication. Author David Brock, who worked on the Troopergate story as a tabloid journalist, said that, for Troopergate, the U.S. right-wing wanted "the imprimatur of a first-rate mainstream news organization," and, by

---

1   By 1998 journalist Michael Kelly would be notorious for his part in what has been called "the most sustained fraud in modern journalism." (*Vanity Fair,* September 1988) Kelly was senior editor at The New Republic during the Stephen Glass scandal. Kelly tacitly admits that 27 of the 41 articles he wrote for *The New Republic* were fabricated in whole or in part.

2   "Saint Hillary" appeared less than three weeks after Bill Clinton and Al Gore announced their cost-cutting *National Performance Review,* May 23, 1993, in a blunting of what had been conservatives' main weapon issue against liberals – government waste.

3   Two months later, in June 1993 (possibly in response to the Times' piece), political scientist Shelley Burtt argued that only a privately oriented politics of civic virtue had both legitimacy and promise. "Despite their differences…two current politics of virtue (liberal and republican), (1) [they] are both publicly oriented and (2) their problems lie in this public orientation."

having the tabloid *Spectator* print it first, they were able to get that imprimatur.[4] The tactic worked so well that it became a major strategic weapon, and a rallying point in the Republican Party propaganda campaigns of the 1990s.

Brock described the new strategy.

> Get a tabloid as backup, for if a major publication fails. When the tabloid publishes, the major will have to follow.[5]

This "Spectator strategy" would endure long past Troopergate – indeed until the present day – and its funding pattern was set long before Troopergate. For the 20 years previous to Troopergate, ultra-right-wing billionaire Richard Mellon Scaife had funded anti-communist propaganda for Ronald Reagan's CIA[6] and published it in his mainstream newspaper, the *Pittsburgh Tribune*.

In the 1990s, with CIA-asset credentials, Scaife gave more than $2 million to fund the "Arkansas Project," an ongoing political vendetta against Bill and Hillary Clinton, run by *The American Spectator* magazine. Scaife's generous contribution paid detectives and reporters to put a microscope on the Clintons and tie them to crimes, real or imagined.[7] These Scaife agents included David Brock,[8] who at the time was a friend of Matt Drudge and Andrew Breitbart of the Internet gossip column *The Drudge Report*.

Soon to be known as "the shouting voice of anti-Clintonism,"[9] *The American Spectator* featured Brock's "Troopergate" story in its January 1994 issue. Days later, the mainstream metro daily *Los Angeles Times* reran the story, and on, and on it went.Next, the tactic of generating mainstream news reports from rumor was used against *Newsweek* magazine. In 1998, with Monica Lewinsky's name surfaced in print for the first time on the tabloid Internet site, *The Drudge Report*. It was *rumored*, the item said, that *Newsweek* magazine had the dirt on Lewinsky's allegations of an affair with Bill Clinton – but was sitting on it.

Two days later, on January 21, 1998, several national media organs turned the Drudge rumor into mainstream news with "Intern Alleges Affair with President" stories.

4   David Brock, *Blinded by the Right*, Crown Press, 2002.
5   Ibid.
6   This was a major CIA propaganda effort during the 1970s. It began as Forum World Features, a news feature service in London whose stories were bought by the *Washington Post*. In 1973, Scaife bought Kern House Enterprises, a US firm that ran *Forum World Features*. Robert Parry; ConsortiumNews.com Web site.
7   Murray Waas, "Behind the Clinton cocaine smear," Salon.com, 2000.
8   Ibid to 4.
9   *The Atlantic*, November 2001.

Later in 1998, Hillary Clinton charged that, largely through the media, a "vast, right-wing conspiracy" was warring against her husband. Later, right-wing TV pundit Ann Coulter confirmed a conspiracy against Clinton, saying humorously,

> It was a small, intricately knit right-wing conspiracy – and I'd like that clarified.[10]

Genuinely humorous, Coulter's remark nevertheless was no joke. Troopergate reporter David Brock, appearing on CNN's *Crossfire*, March 10, 1998, said,

> There is a right-wing (apparatus), I know what it is, I've been there, I was part of it, and yes, they were trying to bring down Bill Clinton by damaging him personally... by any means necessary.

In this confirmed conspiracy, attested to by the hard-right-winger Coulter and the former right-wing operative Brock, the record shows that other assets included Monica Lewinsky, Linda Tripp, and Lucianne Goldberg. Directing the operation, the record suggests, were members either of the CIA itself or, more likely, the familiar operatives from NE-CIA. According to the first elected Russian President, Boris Yeltsin, he learned from his spies that American "right-wing activists" had planted an attractive young woman in the White House as bait to seduce the easily aroused President and throw him into a politically disastrous scandal.[11]

MONICA LEWINSKY

Before Monica Lewinsky went to work in the White House, she announced to friends her intent to seduce Bill Clinton, and she accomplished that seduction. It is asked and answered that there was a sexual affair conducted in the Oval Office, between Ms. Lewinsky and Bill Clinton, beginning perhaps as early as 1995. In April 1996, Lewinsky left the White House for a job at the Pentagon.

LINDA TRIPP

In that Pentagon office, Lewinsky was befriended by fellow worker Linda Tripp and eventually confided details of her affair with the president,

---

10   *The Hartford Courant*, June 25, 1999.
11   Although no one could prove it false, Yeltsin's claim was summarily dismissed by the U.s> mainstream newspapers, using the age-old fallacy of attacking the person making the claim – referring bluntly to Yeltsin as a drunk. Boris Yeltsin, *Midnight Diaries*, Orion Publishing Group, 2001. Yeltsin said his agents had been intrigued not by sex in the White House but by evidence that a conspiracy was acting against the American president. Yeltsin added he did not inform Clinton – whom he admired – of what his agents had reported because he decided Clinton could handle the matter himself.

which apparently was ongoing at least through the end of 1996. Surreptitiously, Tripp caught Lewinsky's account on a concealed mini-recorder. Clearly, Tripp was spying for someone when she did so.

Says Linda Rose Tripp,

> I've worked on the covert side of the Department of Defense. The nature of this position is classified."[12]

Tripp worked for a time at Fort Meade, Maryland, headquarters of the National Security Agency and the Defense Information Systems Agency. There, Tripp aided covert Army Delta Force operations and had official clearance to handle highly classified Army intelligence.[13]

Next, under President George Herbert Walker Bush, Tripp was an intelligence employee at the White House. Because the CIA and the Pentagon have a history of placing intelligence operatives in low-level staff positions at the White House, it is likely Tripp was placed there because polls showed that in the coming 1992 election, a Democrat was likely to defeat former CIA director GHW Bush. That Democrat turned out to be Bill Clinton.

LUCIANNE GOLDBERG

In the 1990s, Lucianne Goldberg was probably the best-known, best-connected American purveyor of low journalism.[14] People pushing "Troopergate" contacted her about publishing allegations by Arkansas state troopers of Clinton's "womanizing" while he served as governor.

Linda Tripp, after "befriending" Lewinsky through their Pentagon jobs, took Lewinsky's private account of her sexual relations with Clinton to Goldberg, who reportedly told Tripp to tape-record future conversations, draw out Lewinsky's tale, and turn it over to Goldberg; which Tripp proceeded to do. Despite a veneer of plausibility as nothing but "vigorous tabloid journalism", it is extremely likely these remarkable actions by Tripp and Goldberg were set up by NE-CIA.

Goldberg, through her chum Victor Lasky, was "friends of friends" with CIA director William Casey, who ran Lasky while he handled public relations for the CIA's "Radio Liberty" propaganda outlet.[15]

The record suggests that the overall intent of this "small, intricately knit right-wing conspiracy" was to dissociate for Americans the historically linked ideas of virtue/character and truth – by setting up the supposedly

---

12   *New York Times*, January 26, 1998.
13   *Washington Post*, Jan 23, 1998.
14   Goldberg hit it big with *Madame Cleo's Girls*, a 1992 novel about a trio of high-class prostitutes.
15   Ibid. to 12

virtue-claiming Clintons and then knocking them down – by catching the then-American leader, Bill Clinton, in a lie and then using a notable and strategic influence over media to publicize that lying. This was the first defeat for Americans' ability to require truth. If their leaders didn't speak the truth, then what?

This doubt contributed to a situation in which, for the first time in America, presidential candidates ceased talking about the truth-related ideas of virtue and character. G.W. Bush did not, Obama did not,[16] and Hillary Clinton during her 2016 campaign did not.[17]

That left it to the US left wing to refurbish the ideal of truth – but in the wake of the trashing of the Clintons, the ideal of truth had to be refurbished in a way not explicitly related to virtue/character. The vehicle that emerged for this was "freedom of information." The new ideal of truth as free flow of information was championed by computer hackers.

---

16   Except for condemning some moral outrage by saying, "That's not who we are. We're better than that."

17   She got as far as calling for "a place for everybody."

CHAPTER 18

THE WAR ON WIKILEAKS

After Lewinsky-gate, and a resulting impeachment vote on Bill Clinton, Matt Drudge told big crowds he'd tapped "a hunger for unedited information." Ironically, another version of "unedited information" would make a second man even more notorious than Drudge: Julian Assange, founder of WikiLeaks.

In the early 1990s, left-wing computer hackers championed "freedom of information," defined as leaks of data filched from corporate and government computer systems. Backlash greeted those efforts. As years passed and WikiLeaks was founded, this right-wing backlash focused increasingly on Assange.

THE WAR ON WIKILEAKS[1]

Today, all that has saved Assange from prison is the government of Ecuador, which, under President Rafael Correa, in August 2012 granted Assange political asylum in Ecuador's London embassy. For years there, Assange had connection to the outside world through telephone and Internet. But US intelligence agents mounted a campaign to unseat the leftist Correa. Many Londoners rallied around Assange, including a British historian, Craig Murray.

Datelined Quito, Ecuador, the South American news service *Andes* reported on October 22, 2016,

> The ex-ambassador of the United Kingdom to Uzbekistan, Craig Murray, informed this Monday that the Central Intelligence Agency of the United States (CIA) invested $87 million with the intent to bring down the Ecuadorian president (Rafael Correa).

In late March 2018, Correa's successor, Lenin Moreno, under U.S. pressure, ordered a cut-off of Assange's telephone and Internet service in the Ecuadoran embassy. Journalist John Pilger commented,

> They cut off the communications for Julian just a day after Ecuador welcomed a delegation from the US Southern Command, the Pentagon's arm in Latin America...[2]

---

1   March 27, 2010 in Salon magazine
2   ConsortiumNews Web site, "On the Silencing of Julian Assange," April 5, 2018.

In the early 1990s, Assange antagonized the American intelligence establishment. He hacked the computers of the Pentagon's Security Coordination Center, saying at the time that militaries, spy agencies, and transnational corporations had become unaccountable, capricious "forms of governance," which, as such, deserved to be hacked.

On his blog, IQ.org, Assange wrote,

> The more secretive or unjust an organisation is, the more that leaks induce fear and paranoia in its leadership and planning coterie… Since unjust systems by their nature induce opponents, and in many places barely have the upper hand, mass leaking leaves them exquisitely vulnerable to those who seek to replace them with more open forms of governance.[3]

CIA director John Deutsch made a thinly veiled reference to Assange as CNN television announced on May 23, 1996: "Cyberspace attacks threaten national security, CIA chief says."

In October 1996, Assange founded WikiLeaks to publish material from other hackers. The site exposed telephone-voice-data harvesting technology patented by the National Security Agency.

> This patent should worry people, [Assange wrote on August 10, 1999]. Everyone's overseas phone calls are or may soon be tapped, transcribed, and archived in the bowels of an unaccountable foreign spy agency.[4]

On September 9, 2007, Wikileaks published classified Pentagon documents about "improvised explosive devices" (IEDs) and their effect on soldiers.[5] The IEDs' typical effect is maiming. The WikiLeak exposed the fact that 30,000 U.S. soldiers were maimed in southwest Asian wars between 2003 and 2010 – suffering limbs blown off and lifelong disability, but that the Pentagon classed these devasting wounds simply as "non-fatal injuries,"[6] like stepping on a piece of glass.

Soon after, the spy division of the U.S. Army proposed arrest and jail for *all WikiLeaks site visitors*.[7] This likely came at the request of brother

---

3   The Guardian.com Jan 30, 2011.
4   Suelette Dreyfus, "This is just between us (and the spies)," The Independent November 15, 1999. The patent uses a method by which a computer automatically assigns a label, or topic description, to raw data and pulls up documents based on their meaning, not just their keywords. This is a notable presaging of Edward Snowden's leak of NSA phone-spying.
5   *The New York Sun*, "Wikileaks Releases Secret Report on Military Equipment"
6   Report compiled by icasualties.org, cited by Ryan Jaroncyk, "After nearly a decade of war, PTSD is afflicting the U.S. military," Civil Rights, May 10, 2010.
7   Its "Counterintelligence Center"; Canvas, June 4, 2010.

spies in the CIA, which agency helped fake the evidence to justify the unnecessary war that killed a few hundred thousand Iraqis and Afghanis, and put those almost 5,000 dead and 30,000 maimed American soldiers in harm's way. As Assange publicized in a 2010 WikiLeaks reported by the *New York Times*:

> The CIA has expanded paramilitary operations inside Afghanistan. The units launch ambushes, order airstrikes, and conduct night raids.[8]

Not surprisingly, after this leak, Assange received threats.[9] Because he knew these were serious threats made by ruthless men who routinely killed for the sake of national security, Assange uprooted himself from any permanent dwelling and drifted around the world, spending most of this time in Sweden.

FRAME IN SWEDEN

Around the same time Assange as a boy had hacked multi-national telecom giant Nortel's Melbourne office computers, a group of Swedish hackers were arrested for invading other multi-national telecom computers. Companies who were hacked joined forces and filed suit in Sweden against this international hacking society of which Assange was a member. Prosecutor Bo Skarinder was to handle the case.

Seemingly as a result, on Sept. 19, 1996, from Sweden, hackers invaded the CIA home Internet page, which, on that day, greeted visitors with: "Welcome to the Central Stupidity Agency – STOP LYING BO SKARINDER."[10]

In 2010 in Sweden, Assange was charged with crimes. The record suggests the CIA was behind this.

In Stockholm on August 14, 2010, Assange had a speaking engagement at the Christian Association of Social Democrats.[11] He needed a place to stay and received word that a particular young Social Democrat would lend him her temporarily vacant apartment.

On August 20, 2010, tabloid newspapers reported that accusations had come against Assange by the tenant of the apartment and a friend of hers. This report was misleading.

---

8   July 25, 2010.

9   *The Guardian*, Friday, 8 January 2010.

10   CNN, Sept. 19, 1996. In response, the CIA said nothing more than that several international telecommunications companies, including one based in Sweden, had pressed charges against hackers, and that Skarinder was lead prosecutor in the case.

11   An organization whose vocal and prominent stand against Israeli occupation of Palestine made it a suitable target for infiltration by Western intelligence agents.

Journalist John Pilger, who obtained case documents concerning telephone text-message records and witness statements made by the tenant, Ann Ardin and co-plaintiff Sofia Wilen, reported,

> One of the (text) messages makes clear that one of the women did not want any charges brought against Assange, 'but the police were keen on getting a hold on him.' She was 'shocked' when they arrested him because she only 'wanted him to take (an HIV) test.' She 'did not want to accuse JA of anything' and 'it was the police who made up the charges.' In a witness statement, she is quoted as saying that she had been 'railroaded by police and others around her.'

Three months later, on November 28, 2010, just as WikiLeaks began publishing the first of 250,000 secret U.S. Embassy cables, it was hit by a cyber-attack called "Distributed denial of service" (DDoS),[12] using a malware weapon with capability that was implanted through a co-opted worker's thumb drive. It was of a type pioneered by the CIA and the Israeli Mossad – eventually called Stuxnet – to crash Iranian computers that controlled nuclear-development centrifuges by overloading the computers with incoming messages.[13] Some former and some current Mossad agents can be considered a foreign branch of Not-Exactly-the-CIA.

Israel had been wounded, less than a year earlier, by WikiLeaks, when Assange publicized "a secret Israeli defense database of all illegal settlements [in Palestine], 186 pages with geophysical coordinates and descriptions in Hebrew."[14]

Fittingly, Israel's champion in the U.S. Senate, Joe Lieberman, pressured Web companies such as Amazon and Tableau to cease providing public access to the WikiLeaks site. Lieberman succeeded, as the *Guardian* reported:

> The US struck its first blow against WikiLeaks after Amazon.com pulled the plug on hosting the whistleblowing website in reaction to heavy political pressure.
>
> The company announced it was cutting WikiLeaks off yesterday only 24 hours after being contacted by the staff of Joe Lieberman, chairman of the Senate's committee on homeland security.[15]

---

12   A distributed denial-of-service (DDoS) is an attack in which multiple compromised computer systems assault a target, such as a server, website or other network resource, and cause a denial of service for users of the targeted resource. The flood of incoming messages, connection requests or malformed packets to the target system forces it to slow down or even crash and shut down, thereby denying service to legitimate users or systems.
13   *New York Times*, Jan 15, 2011.
14   WikiLeaks, February 1, 2009.
15   December 1, 2010.

In 2012, Assange said,

> The Internet, our greatest tool for emancipation, has been transformed into the most dangerous facilitator of totalitarianism we have ever seen.[16]

After 2012, Assange lived in political asylum at London's Ecuadorian Embassy. The record shows the War on WikiLeaks persisted during the 2016 U.S. election period, which was marked by a hack of the Democratic National Committee's computer system. In light of the fact that NE-CIA hacked the Iranian computer system through a worker's thumb drive, it is at least somewhat likely the DNC computer system was hacked the same way.

On April 11, 2019, London police were allowed into the Ecuadorian embassy and arrested Assange for failure to appear in court. The Trump administration has demanded extradition of Assange to the U.S. His fate, as of this writing, remains to be seen.

---

16   Assange, *Cyberpunks*, OR Books, 2012.

CHAPTER 19

THE ENABLERS – KALLSTROM, GIULIANI

The notion that "Immigration weakens national security" began to be popularized long before Donald Trump ran for president in 2016. Around 15 years before, former Assistant Director of the FBI, James Kallstrom, who at the time was head of the New York State Office of Public Security, helped introduce and push the theme of anti-immigration toward national prominence.

In 2002, Kallstrom announced that President Bill Clinton was "loosey-goosey" on immigration. "We need better security at the borders," Kallstrom intoned.[1]

The notion of a border wall to block immigration had been around for years among Americans with no political clout. Celebrity mayor Rudy Giuliani of New York City became the first to say it from a solid political platform.

In 2007, when ABC News reported more than 12 million undocumented immigrants living in the United States, Giuliani proposed a new solution.

> That's a lot of people to walk over your border without being identified, [Giuliani said]. We need to know who's in the United States. We need to know everyone who's in the United States that comes in here from a foreign country. To accomplish this, we need a fence. We need a technological fence.[2]

The "secure the border" notion now had two prominent spokesmen, James Kallstrom and Rudy Giuliani. These men had worked together before, in New York City in the early 1970s, when Kallstrom was a fresh FBI agent and Giuliani was a young assistant prosecutor. By 1993, around the World Trade Center bombing, Kallstrom was New York City FBI agent-in-charge. Giuliani was elected NYC mayor while the WTC 1993 bombing investigation was ongoing.

Giuliani's early years as mayor did not go particularly well, but he was still in office in 2001 when, in the wake of 9/11, Giuliani saw his approv-

---

1   FreeRepublic.com Web site, March 5, 2002.
2   Remarks to reporters in Fort Lauderdale, Florida. Quoted on The American Presidency Project Web site, June 2, 2007.

al ratings jump from 36 percent to 79 percent[3] – from political pariah to "America's mayor."

Kallstrom also got an immediate reward from 9/11. On Oct. 10, 2001, New York Governor George Pataki named Kallstrom Senior Advisor to the Governor for Counter-terrorism, a point of contact with the federal Office of Homeland Security. Like Giuliani (and the previously floundering G.W. Bush administration), after 9/11 Kallstrom's political status soared.

In November 2015, with polls showing even the bumbling Ben Carson running ahead of Trump for the Republican nomination, Kallstrom, on Fox News, decried a "migrant stream" [into Europe] "orchestrated to a large extent [by Muslim terrorists]."[4] Just days later, polls of Republican voters showed Trump ahead of Carson.[5]

In mid-2016, critics of candidate Hillary Clinton alleged that FBI Director James Comey soft-pedaled an investigation into Clinton's use of a private e-mail server for official correspondence while secretary of state. Kallstrom became the mouthpiece for a group of unidentified former government agents who, he said, were angry Clinton was not charged with a crime. On Sept. 28, 2016, describing this group and its intentions, Kallstrom said,

> (A) lot of retired agents and a few on the job … feel like they've been stabbed in the back. I think we're going to see a lot more of the facts come out in the course of the next few months. That's my prediction.[6]

One month later, Comey renewed the Clinton probe. Giuliani immediately said "former agents" – the same unnamed group referred to by Kallstrom – told him they pressured Comey successfully into renewing the probe.

Years later, this group of retired government agents is still keeping secret its members' identities.[7] This secrecy is "spun" via right-wing Web sites that allege the group's members "want to testify" against Comey but will only do so if subpoenaed by Congress (a highly unlikely occurrence) in order not to "undermine the system."

For this secret group of former agents, the record suggests strongly that the label Not-Exactly-the-CIA fits them, as Army Lt. Col. Anthony Shaffer alluded to, as follows:

---

3   Wikipedia.
4   Fox News, November 18, 2015.
5   CNN, November 23, 2015.
6   Daily Beast Web site, November 2, 2016.
7   Cf. PatrioticViralNews.com Web site, June 2018.

a conspiracy of retired intelligence workers, unhappy about Clinton's handling of her State Department e-mails.[8]

James Kallstrom and Rudy Giuliani are unofficial spokesmen for this NE-CIA group with its message "immigration is a danger." Even if, as widely predicted, Trump had lost, this message of anti-immigration was planted in the American-conservative mind – through Twitter and its built-in facilitation of "bots."

---

8   Raffi Khatchadourian, "Man Without a Country," *New Yorker Magazine*, August 21, 2017.

CHAPTER 20

LINEAGE OF CONCEALMENT

A covert operation – in its nature – is a lie.
–Lt. Col. Oliver North,
testifying to Congress, July 10, 1987.

Between World War II and the present, a tremendous amount of U.S. "history" has been made without it being recorded in mainstream history books. This unrecorded history is the sum total of countless covert, often illegal and anti-democratic operations, about which their agents and architects have lied continuously when forced to testify – to keep intact the concealment.

Some Americans, including "Ollie" North, seem to have been more interested than others, or just more active than others, in doing and concealing world-altering deeds from the rest of us. It's almost as if there is a blood-lineage down the years connecting such concealment-minded men.

This "lineage" will continue to procreate and to act. The future will consist partly of covert actions by such men as we have discussed in this book – and "their heirs and assigns."

During the Vietnam war, CIA agent Ted Shackley and naval officer Richard Armitage ran the CIA's covert Operation Phoenix. Armitage raised money for the operation by arranging protection for opium/heroin deals for Lao General Vang Pao.[1] After war's end, under President Gerald Ford, George

---

[1] Court affidavit of Daniel Sheehan, in Avirgan v. Hull, 691 F.Supp. 1357 (SDFla.1988). Sourcing the Sheehan affidavit were former CIA agent Carl Jenkins and former military investigator Gene Wheaton. Jenkins worked under Ted Shackley beginning in 1969, when Shackley was placed in charge of the CIA secret war in Laos. Jenkins became CIA Plans/Programs/Budget Management Officer in Laos. Sheehan's affidavit said, "From late 1973 until April of 1975, Theodore Shackley… and Richard Armitage disbursed, from the secret, Laotian-based, Vang Pao opium fund, vastly more money than was required to finance even the highly intensified Phoenix Project in Vietnam." Also cf. Jonathan Kwitny, Crimes of Patriots, W.W. Norton and Co. 1987. Sheehan's affidavit pulled no punches about the Contra organizers I have called Not-Exactly-the-CIA:

"Defendants, some of whom have been tagged by the press as "contrapreneurs," represent the very epitome of organized crime, but on an international stage. They deal wholesale in narcotic drugs, illegal weapons and violence. Rather than take over local businesses or undermine local government, they seek to take over whole nations. They do not hesitate to murder and destroy anyone or anything that gets in their way. By any definition, these Defendants, alleged merchants

H.W. Bush was CIA director from 1976 to 1977, when, after the election of President Jimmy Carter, Bush was replaced and Shackley was fired.

At this point, Shackley and Armitage had access to surplus money from Operation Phoenix.[2] Shackley, now a private citizen, still had his CIA contacts. With these assets, Shackley and Armitage "privatized" a covert operation – akin to the agency's Operation Phoenix in Iran – that killed opponents of the Shah (conveniently termed communists and terrorists).[3]

Run by ex-CIA Shackley and US naval officer Armitage, this private Iran operation is a fine, early example of Not-Exactly-the-CIA. Note that, also at this time, former CIA director G.H.W. Bush was (newly) outside the agency.

Coincidentally or not, it was at this time that Dick Cheney entered U.S. national politics, as a congressman from Wyoming, while attorney Bill Casey likely was lawyering a Wackenhut arms venture with the Cabazon Indians.

In 1980, Bush Sr. and Ted Shackley met numerous times.[4] Just a few months later, Bush would be vice president and William Casey would be CIA director.

In December 1985, the Iran-Contra plot, hatched among members of NE-CIA, *was* a perfect circle of concealment: *Israel* ships weapons to Iran, the U.S. resupplies *Israel*, and *Israel* pays the United States.[5] As a kicker, the U.S. then used the secret money to fund the Nicaraguan Contra army. Col. North told Congress he thought it was a "neat idea." Furthering this, Shackley's friend Richard Armitage met with Israeli Gen. Menachem Meron, according to a classified Israeli report provided to the Iran-Contra panels.[6]

In 1989, with full knowledge of this, President G.H.W Bush, the ex-CIA director, wanted to appoint Armitage to a cabinet post. But, likely advised by Secretary of Defense Richard Cheney, Armitage declined. Why? The *New York Times* reported,

> Richard L. Armitage, President Bush's choice as Secretary of the Army, withdrew his name from consideration today rather than undergo confirmation hearings expected to include questions about his role in the Iran-Contra affair.[7]

---

of heroin and terrorism, are organized criminals on a scale larger-than-life." Filed on December 12, 1986 (Minor Revisions January 31, 1987).

2 Ibid.
3 Spartacus Educational Web site.
4 Ibid.
5 Wikipedia.
6 *New York Times*, May 26, 1989.
7 Ibid.

Two years later, in 1991, possibly rewarding Armitage for keeping mum, Bush and Cheney named him to "oversee U.S. aid programs" in the former Soviet Union. As such, Armitage helped create a new ruling class in Russia – the mafia-garchs.

Later, on July 14, 2003, Armitage was the go-to man for Vice President Cheney, helping him harm anti-Iraq-war voice Joseph Wilson by "outing" Wilson's wife, Valerie Plame, as a CIA agent.[8] At that point, Armitage's days in public service were numbered. During this time, under pressure from Cheney/Bush/Armitage, the *New York Times* had knowledge of – but did not publish– an important fact: After 9/11, the administration's NSA illegally accessed Americans' phone calls through AT&T.

The *Times* concealed this crime for Cheney, Bush, and Armitage for more than two years, until December 16, 2005. At that time, Armitage's heir and successor as Cheney's right-hand man had been in place for six weeks. This was John Hannah,[9] who had just left the Washington Institute on Near East Policy. Shortly, the Institute urged clandestine warfare (Ted Shackley's formula for success) against Iran, an idea likely cooked up by Hannah. Soon, legalizing the NSA spying on Americans became a priority. In February 2008, with Hannah a foundation advisor, the Foundation for Defense of Democracies[10] helped Cheney and Bush push through legislation to legalize and maintain the NSA's phone-spying system.

With Hannah on board, the FDD has been referred to as the No. 1 outside influence on President Donald Trump. Major FDD donors include casino magnate Sheldon Adelson and Bernard Marcus – the second-biggest donor to Trump's campaign in 2016.

Special prosecutor Robert Mueller probed: "Cheney alums' persistent presence in American domestic politics (and their) doing things outside customary boundaries."[11]

---

8   FOX News October 29, 2014 Cheney advisor Scooter Libby was blamed for outing Plame, but in fact it was Armitage, the more experienced Cheney advisor, who did it. In their book Hubris, Michael Isikoff and David Corn reveal – as both Armitage and syndicated columnist Robert Novak acknowledged publicly later – that Armitage was Novak's "initial" and "primary source" for Novak's July 2003 column that revealed Plame's identity as a CIA operative. On September 7, 2006, Armitage admitted to being the source in the Plame CIA leak. A month later, Armitage was out of public service, lobbying the Taiwanese government on behalf of a US surveillance-equipment company.

9   The Guardian October 10, 2012. Hannah, in coming years, would also serve private right-wing groups that advised on foreign policy, including the Washington Institute on Near East Policy.

10   Through a newly founded spin-off affiliate, Defense for Democracies.

11   Prof. Karen Greenberg, head of Fordham Law School's Center for National Security.

Joel Zamel and Erik Prince

As founder Alexander Nix of Cambridge Analytica acknowledged concerning their interference in the 2016 election,

> We use(d) some Israeli companies. From Israel, very effective in intelligence gathering.12

Although Cambridge Analytica closed, this Israeli-tinged espionage apparatus is largely intact and available for rogue intelligence-community meddling in the 2020 U.S. election. As we have seen, the record suggests a group connected to Dick Cheney is part of that apparatus.

Cheney's former national security adviser John Hannah introduced Lebanese George Nader to Israeli Joel Zamel, who presented a spy plan to Donald Trump Jr. and whose PsyGroup company worked with Cambridge Analytica to influence the 2016 election.

At Zamel's other venture, Wikistrat, Cheney's friend Hannah is currently a chief advisor,[13] along with Bush-Cheney national security advisor Elliott Abrams and Michael V. Hayden, a former CIA head.[14]

Former Wikistrat analyst James Kadtke told The *Daily Beast*,

> It was clear to me that… these guys had intelligence backgrounds, intelligence professionals, not academics or analysts… It seemed mysterious… I got the impression they were doing things outside of Wikistrat.

Even to employees, the source of PsyGroup's money has been a mystery. A former employee said,

> Clients paid decently but not enough to sustain the company… We were getting money from somewhere else.[15]

Both the advisors and the funding for Zamel's Wikistrat display the stamp of NE-CIA.[16]

---

12   *Times of Israel* March 20, 2018. A White Knight Holdings Public Company Limited is based in Cyprus, as was PsyGroup. It has been reported, perhaps inaccurately, that Zamel's WhiteKnight is based in the Philippines.

13   Heavy.com Web site November 16, 2018

14   *New York Times* April 4, 2018

15   *The Daily Beast*, June 4, 2018

16   Both Nader and Blackwater founder Erik Prince have worked for the ruler of the United Arab Emirates, Sheik Mohammed bin Zayed. The investigation by special prosecutor Robert Mueller was concerned with an August 2016 meeting – arranged by Prince – among Zamel, Nader, and Donald Trump Jr., which happened after Zamel's PsyGroup wrote a multi-million-dollar plan designed to help Donald Trump, Sr. become president in 2016. Mueller was also concerned with suspect flows of money to PsyGroup at a bank in Cyprus. Cf. New York Times May 19, 2018.

So does Erik Prince, the man who brought Zamel to Donald Trump, Jr. The backgrounds of the two men, Prince and Zamel, are remarkably similar.

PRINCE

B orn in 1969 to Edgar and Elsa Prince, Erik Prince grew up in Holland, Michigan, a conservative Dutch-immigrant enclave.

Young Erik was barely into his teens when Elsa joined the Council for National Policy, a secretive networking group for ultra-conservatives whose members have included Contragate's Lt. Col. Oliver North and Gen. John Singlaub.[17] It is highly likely that as guest of his mother, Elsa, Erik Prince attended CNP meetings during the 1980s, and there met North and Singlaub while the Contra operation was at its height.[18]

In 1992, Prince graduated from Michigan's Hillsdale College,[19] which has a Washington DC annex across the street from The Heritage Foundation, and is known as "The College That Wants to Take Over Washington."[20] The campus hosts regular dinners for members of Congress and their staffs. Prince was a White House intern under Dick Cheney and George W. Bush beginning in 1990, so Hillsdale's Washington DC annex was likely where Prince did a great deal of his college work.

ZAMEL

J oel Zamel's college near Tel Aviv, Interdisciplinary Center Herzliya, shares a campus with the Mossad-linked International Institute for Counter Terrorism. For IDC Herzliya, Bush-Cheney advisor John Hannah has sponsored numerous speakers, including the following:

- Mark Dubowitz, executive director of Foundation for Defense of Democracies, where John Hannah is senior counselor;

- Elliott Abrams, advisor with Hannah to Zamel's Wikistrat and a national security advisor to the Bush-Cheney administration; and

- Mary Beth Long, former CIA agent, assistant secretary of defense in the Bush-Cheney administration.

---

17   Wikipedia.

18   Prince and North, in late 2017, reportedly pitched Trump a plan for a private spy network answering only to Trump. *The Intercept*, "Trump White House Considers Plans for Secret Spy Network," Dec 4, 2017.

19   Hillsdale was promised by Erik's sister Betsy Prince and her husband Dick DeVos, heir to the Amway fortune, that the college could safely dump affirmative action, forego federal money, and convert to "donor support." Hillsdale did so, meaning, effectively, that educations from Hillsdale essentially are underwritten by the very wealthiest of the nation's ultra-right, such as Charles G. Koch; donors who "have never set foot on campus" but who, together, pay one-half or more of Hilldsale's $66,000 tuitions.

20   *Politico* Magazine, May 12, 2018.

IDC Herzliya was modeled after U.S. colleges like Prince's Hillsdale and Harvard College. Back in 1978, news broke that the CIA used Harvard College faculty members for covert operations. CIA spokesman Dale Peterson suggested nothing was wrong with that, saying,

> Basically, what you have are two institutions – Harvard and the CIA – with overlapping interests.[21]

Another model for Zamel's IDC Herzliya was Calvin College in Grand Rapids, Michigan, a city that bears watching as the 2020 U.S. election approaches.

---

21   *Harvard Crimson,* October 11, 1991.

CHAPTER 21

RUSSIAN PLAYERS

ALFA BANK, THE KATSYV FAMILY, MARIIA BUTINA

Some Russians in position to meddle in the 2016 U.S. election and seemingly remaining so for the 2020 election, are Alfa Bank owner Mikhail Fridman, the mafiagarch Katsyv family, and young people like Mariia Butina.

MIKHAIL FRIDMAN AND ALFA BANKSTERS

In the years before the Soviet Union dissolved, the CIA covertly operated two Harvard-allied consultants in Moscow. They helped Anatoly Chubais, the Russian deputy prime minister, write a plan to "privatize" (capitalize) all key Soviet industries in a short time.[1]

When this happened, Mikhail Fridman quickly founded Alfa Bank. At "auction" from the state, Fridman acquired Tyumen oil company, attracting the attention and eventual partnership of oilman Dick Cheney. Cheney visited the U.S. Capitol personally to lobby, against federal objection, for a half-billion dollars in loans to Tyumen and to Cheney's Halliburton from the Ex-Im Bank.[2]

When Tyumen announced the approval of its Ex-Im Bank loan, Cheney attended the news conference,[3] presumably at Tyumen's corporate office in Tyumen, Russia, 1,320 miles from Moscow. But by 2005, Alfa Bank and Fridman were widely viewed as mobbed-up.

According to court documents,

> (A) former KGB major ... said that Alfa Bank was founded with party and KGB funds, and quickly attracted rogue agents who... "quickly determined that dealing in drugs would bring the highest profits, with literally no risk in Russia." [An] FSB report claimed that Alfa Group's top executives, oligarchs Mikhail Fridman and

---

1   Revealed to RIA Novosti. Russian Legal Information Agency, April 25, 2013; *Telesur* March 16, 2018.
2   *Chicago Tribune*, August 10, 2000.
3   Kim Martin, a spokeswoman for Fleischman Hillard, the public relations firm representing Tyumen. Baltimore Sun, August 15, 2000.

Pyotr Aven, "allegedly participated in the transit of drugs from Southeast Asia through Russia and into Europe."[4]

The same FSB document claims that at the end of 1993, a top Alfa Bank official agreed to take money transfers from top cocaine merchants: Colombia's Cali cartel. The FSB document closes by noting that, "Tyumen could have significant access to the White House should the Bush-Cheney ticket win in the November presidential elections." Here perhaps is both the origin – Dick Cheney and mobbed-up Alfa Banksters – and the essential nature – organized crime, pure and simple – of Russian influence in U.S. presidential politics. Even Fridman himself has said,

> The rules of (Russian) business are quite different to western standards.… To say one can be completely clean and transparent is not realistic.[5]

Whether aware of this danger or not, Bill Clinton's Secretary of State Madeline Albright opposed the Ex-Im Bank loans to Fridman's Tyumen and Cheney's Halliburton. But within her department, the CIA, which had to have known Fridman's Alfa Bank reputation, rated Fridman's Tyumen highly in "above-board business practices," according to an Ex-Im attorney who worked on the Tyumen account.[6] For the CIA to give Tyumen a good rating, likely undeserved, makes sense as a help to Cheney, defense secretary under George H.W. Bush and likely to be picked in 2000 by George W. Bush as vice presidential candidate.

Too, though, the CIA's good rating of Tyumen helped its owner Fridman, and so helped Fridman's other company, Alfa Bank. Counting the CIA's helping create "privatization" in Russia in 1991, which helped Fridman's fledgling Alfa Bank, the CIA's good rating of Tyumen in 1999 is the second connection of the Central Intelligence Agency with Alfa Bank. As such, Fridman and other Alfa Banksters, along with the CIA and NE-CIA, deserve a high ranking among forces arrayed against the 2020 election. This is supported by a review of an odd computer connection discovered in 2016 between Alfa Bank and Trump Towers.

---

4   UNITED STATES DISTRICT COURT FOR THE DISTRICT OF COLUMBIA OAO ALFA BANK et al., Plaintiffs, v. Civil Action No. 00-2208 (JDB) CENTER FOR PUBLIC INTEGRITY et al., Defendants.
5   Ibid. to 24.
6   Center for Public Integrity August 2, 2000.

PYOTR AND DENIS KATSYV

A main reason the mafiagarch Katsyv family of Russia and Israel is still a possible meddler in the 2020 election is its seeming patronage from Donald Trump.

A US money-laundering suit against the Katsyvs failed to go to trial in 2017 – after President Trump fired the prosecutor. Previously, an Israel money-laundering suit against the Katsyvs – "the biggest money-laundering case in Israel's history" – also failed to go to trial.[7]

In the winter of 2008, $850,000 in an Alfa Bank account was transferred to a Swiss account[8] for a Denis Katsyv company named Prevezon Holdings, an international real estate firm.[9] This money transfer happened around the same time Donald Trump, Jr. told people at a Manhattan real-estate conference that for the Trump empire,

> We see a lot of money pouring in from Russia … Russians make up a pretty disproportionate cross-section of … our assets.

Special Prosecutor Robert Mueller's probe into influence on the 2016 U.S. presidential election was partly concerned with money laundering. On March 11, 2017, barely six weeks past his inauguration, Trump fired the Katsyv case prosecutor, Preet Bharara.[10] The case was still scheduled for trial, but never made it to court.[11]

Writing to Attorney General Jeff Sessions, House Judiciary Committee Democrats said,

> We write with some concern that the two events (the firing of Bharara and the failure to prosecute Katsyv) may be connected – and that the [Attorney General's] Department may have settled the case at a loss for the United States in order to obscure the underlying facts.

---

7   Russia's Katsyv family, with son Denis a dual Russian/Israeli citizen, first was suspected of money laundering in 2005. In Tel Aviv, some 20 employees were arrested at Hapoalim Bank, where customers included Denis Katsyv and leading "oligarchs" from Russia. Police suspected Hapoalim took in foreign crime money and immediately – via "back-to-back" standing orders – transferred it to shell companies. Cf. Haaretz, March 7, 2005.

8   OCCRP Bunicon-Impex SRL and Elenast-Com SR.

9   These funds allegedly were stolen from the Russian tax authority by a ring of organized crime figures and Russian state officials. This became involved in the well-known Magnitsky case.

10   Because Bharara was also probing Deutsche Bank, principal lender to Trump, Trump attorney Marc Kasowitz warned the president, "This guy is going to get you."

11   On the last business day before the trial was to open, on May 12, 2017, the case mysteriously settled. The replacement prosecutor, Joon Kim, had not consulted with Attorney General Jeff Sessions before he made the settlement. Katsyv once again avoided being questioned in court. A scheduled witness immediately asked whether "political pressure" had been brought to prevent court testimony.

On November 7, 2018, immediately following the Democratic take-over of Congress in the mid-term elections, Trump fired Sessions.

Mariia Butina

Butina, with her good looks and gun-girl persona, had great appeal to the NRA and other Republicans. She appears to have had some influence, possibly quite small, on American politics before the 2016 election. As of her arrest and eventual sentencing on April 26, 2019, to 18 months' imprisonment, this influence is over. But it bears looking at the source, in case others of Butina's ilk emerge in front of the 2020 election. Butina's record shows a connection to Russian mafia-connected Alfa Bank. The record suggests Mariia Butina is not a government spy, but is simply plain Russian mafia, a vigorous opportunist. However, in Russia (and, for that matter, in numerous other countries), the line between elected government and organized crime is often so thin as to become virtually invisible.

Butina said in 2017 that her gun group was funded by billionaire Konstantin Nikolaev. This appears incomplete. A spokesperson for Nikolaev told Radio Free Europe,

> [Nikolaev] briefly provided some funding to the organization, from 2012 to 2014, [but] has had no contact with Ms. Butina or her organization since 2014.[12]

Who funded Butina's years of travel in America during 2015 and 2016? Butina grew up in Barnaul, a city of 600,000 in Russia's poorest area, Altai Krai, in southwestern Siberia, an area in which events point to influence by the Russian mafia:

- In 2002, a Barnaul resident handled ransom money in a kidnapping and murder in the U.S. of five affluent emigres from Russia. The FBI visited Barnaul to detain and question the man.[13]

- In 2003, Russian authorities got information on a thieves' gathering in Moscow at which was discussed control over mob activities in Altai Krai.

- Also, in 2003, Barnaul Mayor Vladimir Bavarin died in a suspect car crash.

- In 2005, the governor of Altai Krai, Mikhail Evdokimov, died in another suspect car crash.[14]

---

12   Radio Free Europe Web site, July 26, 2018.
13   *Moscow Times*, April 30, 2004.
14   Wikipedia.

• From 2012 to 2014, Maxim Savintsev, son of another Barnaul mayor, was noted to be leading an organized-crime group,[15] after fraudulently gaining control of a city-connected company[16] and allegedly stealing 19 million rubles.

And, in Butina's home town, the Barnual Cartridge Co. made ammunition – some of it for handguns not legal for civilians to own in Russia – including the Luger 9mm, the Makarov 9mm, and the Colt .45. The government shut down Barnaul Cartridge in February 2010, for illegal sales of cartridges to civilians.[17] Very likely, the lawbreaking civilian customers of Barnaul Cartridge were mobsters. Further, it seems probable that much of the short supply of money in Barnaul was controlled by the mob.

Butina needed money to visit Moscow, found a faux gun club, and travel to the US. According to the *Daily Beast*, a public-relations expert named Igor Pisarsky was bagman for money going to Butina.[18] Pisarsky worked in the "private-client" division of Alfa Bank, serving only wealthy customers. As we shall review later in this chapter, Alfa's private-client division has long been known for serving wealthy mobsters.

Butina has said she worked as a journalist. She has also said that she owned "several" furniture stores in Barnaul. This seems suspect for a journalist in poverty-ridden Altai Krai. Butina has added that selling the Barnaul stores got her the money to move to Moscow – a distance of 2,230 miles – and to found 'Right to Bear Arms'. This *all* seems suspect; from where, most likely, did the money come? Mobsters, more than any other demographic sector, are inconvenienced by Russia's ban on civilian handgun ownership. It is easy to imagine a mobbed-up Barnaul as the kind of place where people like to flaunt firearms – with women who "lock and load" regarded as sex symbols.

It seems fair to say Butina used her charm and the dangerous allure of firearms to cultivate a sexy image on her personal Web site. A Web address that previously featured Butina's personal Web site now advertises pornography.[19]

It is widely supposed that Butina and "Right to Bear Arms" acted in the U.S. as agents of Russian President Vladimir Putin. But "Right to Bear

15   en.sledcom.ru/news, August 7, 2015.
16   Ministry of Internal Affairs of the Russian Federation Web site, February 11, 2015.
17   With Russian Ministry of Interior Order N85 of February 3, 2010, which handed down a "major government license suspension" for "gross violations of the manufacture and supply of ammunition, including civilians, prohibited trafficking in the territory of Russia (that) violated the Federal Law of 13/12/96 'On Weapons.'"
18   August 9, 2018.
19   Radio Free Europe Web site, July 26, 2018.

Arms" itself has denied this, with the group's most recent deputy head, Vyacheslav Vaneyev, calling the notion, "Complete stupidity."[20]

In 2018, Right to Bear Arms ran out of money, failed to file accounting paperwork, and was liquidated by a Russian court. Vaneyev said, "If we were a Kremlin project, they certainly wouldn't have closed us. We would have [had] a certain amount of financing."

It is supposed that Butina's friend Alexander Torshin, a one-time government minister, was a pipeline between Butina and Russian President Vladamir Putin. But Vladimir Milov, an opposition politician in Russia for whom Butina spoke at a rally in 2011, said,

> I don't think that these people (Butina and Torshin) ever had any illusion that the gun issue could be promoted to the top of Russian politics.[21]

Indeed, the powerful Putin opposes a right to bear arms in Russia. As Russia's prime minister, Putin said in 2011,

> I am deeply convinced that the free flow of firearms will bring a great harm and represents a great danger for us.[22]

At the 2011 opposition rally at which Butina spoke, Milov said, he was struck by the expensive equipment displayed by 'Right to Bear Arms' and the expensive merchandise they gave away at their rallies. Milov said,

> "There was a clear idea from the beginning that somebody is behind them, big money is behind them."

According to Spanish police, Torshin is a lawyer for the Russian mob.[23] "Right to Bear Arms" had no government funding, and its money from oligarch Nikolaev dried up in 2014. About all that is left is plain old mafia funding for the years 2014 to 2017.

As such, then, Torshin and Butina's U.S. travels in April 2015 seeking both NRA help to loosen gun laws in Russia and increased access to Donald Trump would have been made on behalf of mobsters who wanted handguns as widely available in their country as such weapons are in the

---

20   Ibid.
21   Ibid.
22   Ibid. Despite or because of such evidence, US media reports continued into 2019 that "the Kremlin" either ordered or at least blessed Butina's and Torshin's gun-rights efforts in the US, which included meetings with Naional Rifle Association officials. A January 2019 story quoted two ex-CIA agents to the effect that "the Kremlin" ran Butina as a spy. Cf. the Daily Beast, January 13, 2019.
23   Bloomberg, August 8, 2016.

US and a US leader who would support that change. This theory is supported by the fact of connections of Butina/Torshin/Right to Bear Arms
to Alfa Bank, and Alfa's connection to Trump via an Alfa Bank-Trump
computer link.

CHAPTER 22

ALFA BANK-TRUMP TOWERS-SPECTRUM HEALTH: THE COMPUTER CONNECTIONS

In June 2016, electronics experts discovered that three computer servers were connected among Alfa Bank, Trump Towers, and Spectrum Health.[1] Spectrum is a health-care conglomerate based in Grand Rapids, Michigan that is influenced heavily by the DeVos family through property ties, donations, and board memberships.[2] The DeVos family owns Amway company.

Top officials from Alfa Bank said in 2013 they would invest $2 billion in "American health care" through their newly founded company, LetterOne. As we shall see in later pages, at that time a whopping share of "American health care" investment opportunities were controlled by Amway owners Richard DeVos and Jay Van Andel. Also at that time, Amway contracted with Alfa Bank for an electronic "loyalty card" system to track the purchase credits amassed by Amway's Russian customers.

The FBI investigated computer activity between the Trump organization and Alfa Bank, but did not investigate the computer link between Alfa Bank and Spectrum Health or the computer link between the Trump organization and Spectrum Health.[3]

Money was being transferred, computer scientists believed, among Alfa, Trump, and Spectrum.[4] Another theory was that the computers transferred names and electronic addresses for tens of thousands of Spectrum medical customers – data usable in election meddling in Michigan.[5]

---

1   *New Yorker*, Oct 15, 2018
2   The Helen DeVos Children's Hospital is owned by Spectrum Health, and Spectrum Health Foundation officials include emeritus board member Dick DeVos and vice chair Maria DeVos.
3   Wikipedia
4   *New Yorker* October 8, 2018
5   Ibid. and "Trump Tower's Stealth Russian Data Machine," by the computer scientist using the moniker Tea Pain; Teapainusa.wordpress.com April 3, 2017

I believe the record suggests that both money and personal data of Michigan residents were transferred. This would have served both money laundering and election meddling.[6]

---

6   *Haaretz* September 4, 2018.
In 2007, Heartland Payments Systems – eventually acquired by DeVos-linked Global Payments -- was breached by accomplices of Alberto Gonzalez, who at the time was under arrest and turned US federal super-informant, giving hacking seminars and conferences to federal agents, showing them how to use his hacking tools. In 2014, Alfa Bank sold to Global Payments the Amway "loyal-ty-card" credit system, thus linking Global Payments both to Amway and by extension to the DeVos family-influenced Spectrum Health conglomerate. Then, in early 2016, the De Vos-linked Global Payments acquired another electronic credit system, from Heartland Payments, that had previous-ly been hacked by accomplices of Albert "SoupNazi" Gonzalez, a federal informant hacking genius, who gave seminars on hacking techniques to federal agents.
Gonzalez said,
          "These presentations were attended by at least 50 Secret Service agents and
          by a number of persons who were not (Secret Service) agents."
Those who were not Secret Service agents – but who necessarily had equal security clearance to that of the Service –likely were with the CIA and other US intelligence agencies and thus, Not-Ex-actly-CIA, too, was positioned to have Gonzalez's hacking expertise and to have the capability of hacking electronic credit-payment systems – and thus to have capability to use credit-payment systems to launder money. It is interesting to ponder whether, after banks were exposed as arrant money launderers by an American employee of a Swiss bank, in 2007, international money laun-derers began washing money through hacked credit-payment systems.

CHAPTER 23

MARSHALING THE ANTI-IMMIGRATION VOTE

H istorically, right-wing zealots have feared that a string of Democrat presidents would threaten national security.

In the run-up to the 2016 presidential election, Democrat Barack Obama had governed for nearly eight years and Democrat Hillary Clinton was a strong candidate to succeed him. The record shows right-wing zealots in Shackleyesque fashion saw a need to fight, covertly, this prospective string of Democrat presidencies.

The issue of immigration was a weapon ready-made. Already, a small block of U.S. voters believed immigration should be slowed or stopped. With the help of Cambridge Analytica, as was widely reported, a powerful right-wing bloc swayed voters to believe in "protecting" the country from immigration.[1]

Tactic: Exploit Internet Social Network Systems

I nventors of Facebook did little research on unintended consequences of the product before launching it in 2004. But eventually, Facebook researcher Adam Kramer published a startling finding: *Facebook transferred one person's emotion to other people.* Kramer called this effect "mass (emotional) contagion."[2] Kramer counted emotionally "positive" and emotionally "negative" posts being made by Facebook friends. He wrote,

> After a user makes a status update with emotional content, their friends are significantly more likely to make (an emotion-) consistent post.... Emotion spreads via ... communications media.

---

1   Even if Donald Trump had not been elected, a vocal anti-immigration base would have allowed constant carping against any Democrat who defeated him – a carping designed to destabilize that Democrat presidency, as Bill Clinton's presidency had been destabilized by Not-Exactly-the-CIA with Troopergate and Monica Lewinsky.

2   Adam Kramer, "The Spread of Emotion via Facebook," Proceedings of the SIGCHI Conference on Human Factors in Computing Systems, Austin, Texas, May 5, 2012; cf. also Kramer et al, , "Experimental Evidence Of Massive-Scale Emotional Contagion Through Social Networks, *Proceedings of the National Academy of Sciences of the United States of America*, June 2, 2014.

Researchers said the study results were significant.

> In a domain as large as Facebook, if expressing [anger] on one day causes one out of 100 friends to post [angrily] three days later, then the tens of millions of people posting each day may be responsible for hundreds of thousands of [angry] posts that would not have otherwise occurred, and which in turn could cause thousands more; we do not consider this trivial.[3]

Studies have shown that around political issues, users of Internet social networking become averse to talking things over rationally in face-to-face discussion.[4] As it happens, a Pentagon "psy-ops" (psychological operations) team is interested in making people averse to using reasoning.

For more effective psy-ops, researchers said, the Pentagon needs

> "Narratives that influence listeners in a way that overrides conventional reasoning in the context of morally questionable actions."[5]

Kramer's study proved empirically that messages via Facebook could override reasoning.[6] Facebook was a tool waiting to be used in psy-ops.

The record shows this tool was used to influence US voters. In 2016, a company advertising "use (of) data to change audience behavior," Cambridge Analytica, exploited Facebook.[7]

The *Guardian* describes the role of Cambridge Analytica in the US election as follows:

> "The idea ... was to bring big data and social media to an established military methodology – 'information operations' – then turn it on the US electorate."[8]

Who ordered this psy-op? The finding that Facebook could override reasoning was a boon for Not-Exactly-the-CIA. A member of the Psychometrics Centre told the *Guardian*,

---

3   Ibid.

4   Antonio and Hanna Damasio, who are principal investigators in the 'Neurobiology of Narrative Framing' project at the University of Southern California.

5   DARPA-funded scientists reporting on their "Neurobiology of Narrative Framing" project – Pentagon Highlands Forum, 2011.

6   Everything indicates Kramer and fellow researchers did not intend this.

7   *New York Times*, March 17, 2018, "How Trump Consultants Exploited the Facebook Data of Millions"

8   March 18, 2018, "I made Steve Bannon's psychological warfare tool: Meet the data war whistleblower"

"Agencies that fund research on behalf of the intelligence services...were all over this research."[9]

Funding for this research came from then-co-owner of Breitbart News Robert Mercer. Many Cambridge Analytica campaign messages for Trump were anti-Muslim.[10] Helping Trump's 2016 campaign, Cambridge Analytica broke the law. This was admitted by the company's CEO, Alexander Nix, on a secret videotape aired by British television.[11] The Trump campaign for 2020 is employing both former Cambridge Analytica head of product Matt Oczkowski and former Cambridge Analytica chief of data science David Wilkinson.[12]

---

9   Apparently at the urging of DARPA, weapons contractor Boeing funded Kosinski's PhD research.

10   On Facebook feeds, voters saw, for example, a travel ad of a Frenchwoman welcoming visitors to the "Islamic State of France," where "under Sharia law, you can enjoy everything the Islamic State of France has to offer, as long as you follow the rules." As the video opens, missiles are seen flying through the sky. Blindfolded men appear, kneeling, with guns pointed at their heads. Children train with weapons, "to defend the caliphate."

11   London-based Channel 4 News, March 19, 2018. On the tape, Nix said Cambridge Analytica "ran all of (Donald Trump's) digital campaign" and boasted of using prostitutes, "honey traps," and bribery-sting operations to discredit politicians – while being paid ostensibly for merely doing research on these candidates.

12   Associated Press, June 15, 2018

CHAPTER 24

WHAT IS ARRAYED AGAINST FUTURE U.S. ELECTIONS?

SWING STATE – MICHIGAN

In 1976, the large conglomerate Advance Publications acquired nearly every newspaper of size in Michigan. Among these were the *Flint Journal* (serving a racially divided city), the *Saginaw News*, and the *Bay City Times*. These three Advance-owned papers hit subscriber porches just before the 2008 election wrapped with a message paid for by the National Rifle Association: "Defend America – Defeat Obama."[1]

Today, all of the Advance-owned newspapers feed an "MLive" Web site run by Advance. Almost each day, a story on MLive carries the name DeVos, or Van Andel, or Spectrum Health, typically using congratulatory language such as "community partnership" and "innovation."

In Grand Rapids, Michigan, Richard DeVos (Erik Prince's uncle-in-law) and fellow CIA asset Jay Van Andel, over decades through their Amway company, built a political empire that, through ongoing, massive campaign contributions has influenced Michigan governors and legislators. In recent years, the ante is upped – now, a DeVos-Van Andel combine apparently wants to influence presidential elections – by importing conservative voters to Michigan.[2]

A NATIONAL-SECURITY ZONE

Engineering conservatism in Michigan is nothing new. Anti-union business practice was brutally enforced there before and during World War II by Henry Ford. Michigan was where Ford produced aircraft and Louis Chevrolet made Sherman tanks. Hired by Ford, a private thug army hospitalized organizers who would have unionized his factory.[3]

---

1   *Flint Journal*, November 3, 2008. The newspaper blamed its newspaper carriers, saying they mistakenly wrapped the paper in what was supposed to have been an insert.

2   Betsy DeVos has stated flatly her intent to use family wealth to "win elections."

3   "The Service Department," Ford's 800-man security gang, staffed with "ruffians and criminals," by 1937 was called "the most powerful private police force in the world" as it battered union organizers. MetroTimes Web site May 26, 2015; Military History of the Upper Great Lakes Web site, Oct 12, 2015, and H. L. Mencken's *American Mercury* magazine.

For this work, Ford looked for brawn, but the government wanted brains out of Michigan's security zone, including future Secretary of Defense Robert McNamara, ex-Army Air corpsman and leader at Ford of "The Whiz Kids."

MacNamara's fellow ex-Army Air Force corpsmen in Michigan at the time were Richard DeVos and Jay Van Andel. It is likely the CIA tapped them for a mission to Cuba. In 1949, the boyhood friends sailed a schooner to Cuba just after the Castro brothers, Fidel and Raul, had formed a revolutionary army. It was also at the time when the Dulles brothers, Allen and John (who later would run the CIA and the State Department, respectively), worked for United Fruit Company, which owned 95 percent of Oriente province – Cuba's largest – and the childhood home of the Castro brothers.

In explanation of the voyage, DeVos and Van Andel have said they "were entrepreneurial" and "wanted to see how things were done" outside the U.S. When they pushed off on this voyage, DeVos and Van Andel knew nothing of boats or sailing. Reportedly, they ran aground several times before reaching the Caribbean.

Once there, DeVos and Van Andel said, off the coast of Cuba their boat took on water – because it was caulked badly, a fact that, they said, they hadn't learned while buying the boat. Although implausible on its face, this story, to my knowledge, has not been questioned.

Van Andel and DeVos decided to sink the boat, they said, to remove a danger to other sailors in the area. Somehow, the pair went ashore on Cuba.[4] What Van Andel and DeVos did there is unclear. On the whole – from their connection to the OSS through the Army Air Corps to their postwar presence in security-sensitive Michigan, to their vague and improbable account of the boat voyage – the record suggests strongly that the pair worked in Cuba as spies.

Upon returning to Grand Rapids later in 1949, DeVos and Van Andel became top-selling distributors for Nutrilite, a modified Ponzi-style company destined to lose a false-advertising case brought by the FDA.

While the Nutrilite case dragged slowly through the courts, Michigan State University in 1955 joined the U.S. war effort by contracting to develop, train, and equip the Vietnamese police in a program authorized by University President John A. Hannah, former assistant secretary of defense. Primarily, the Michigan State Advisory Group, which included a

---

4   Several accounts of the peculiar voyage omit this key detail, which was reported in *Yachting Monthly*, February 2008.

unit staffed and funded by the CIA, spent time remaking the *Surete*, Vietnam's intelligence agency left over from the French Colonial era.[5]

In 1959, with Nutrilite destined to lose in court, Van Andel and DeVos essentially stole Nutrilite's "multi-level marketing" idea and started Amway. In a 1975 formal complaint the Federal Trade Commission alleged Amway was a Ponzi scheme. This put in limbo – as FTC proceedings dragged on for years – an empire that was building modern-day Michigan. During these years, Watergate brought down Richard Nixon and Gerald Ford took over as president until January 1977.

That year, Amway bought a national radio network, MBS, into whose broadcasts the CIA had secretly been inserting Radio Free Europe's anti-Soviet propaganda messages. A previous station owner, Fulton Lewis, had discovered and stopped the secret practice.

The following reproduced document, recently declassified, is "CIA RDP7400297R00900090059-3" transcribing an MBS broadcast by Lewis on November 15, 1957:

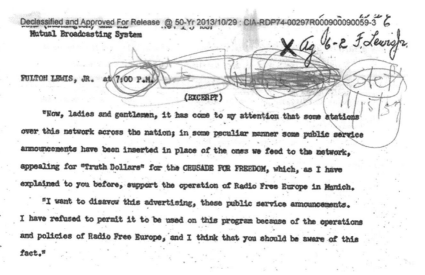

Declassified and Approved For Release @ 50-Yr 2013/10/29 : CIA-RDP74-00297R000900090059-3

Mutual Broadcasting System

FULTON LEWIS, JR. at 7:00 P.M.

(EXCERPT)

"Now, ladies and gentlemen, it has come to my attention that some stations over this network across the nation; in some peculiar manner some public service announcements have been inserted in place of the ones we feed to the network, appealing for "Truth Dollars" for the CRUSADE FOR FREEDOM, which, as I have explained to you before, support the operation of Radio Free Europe in Munich.

"I want to disavow this advertising, these public service announcements. I have refused to permit it to be used on this program because of the operations and policies of Radio Free Europe, and I think that you should be aware of this fact."

So, in 1977, Amway apparently returned to the fold of CIA assets a company, MBS, that the CIA likely was missing for its propaganda purposes.

In spring 1979, the word was out that the FTC would finally rule on whether Amway violated the law.

---

5   Politico, March 25, 2018, referring to Ramparts Magazine's April 1966 story co-written by Warren Hinckle, Robert Scheer, and Sol Stern. Hannah denied that MSU was involved in spying, and then resigned abruptly from MSU in 1969 to become director of the U.S. Agency for International Development, an agency with known ties to the CIA.

But, precisely one week before the final FTC ruling, Jay Van Andel and Richard DeVos traveled on May 1, 1979 to meet at the U.S. Capitol Building with a fellow Grand Rapids native – Gerald Ford, very recently appointed President of the United States.[6] Seven days later, on May 8, 1979, the FTC exonerated Amway.[7]

The DeVos-Van Andel combine would continue to function as a CIA asset. Under Ronald Reagan, in 1984, Van Andel and CIA director William Casey founded the Jamestown Foundation, with Dick Cheney – then a congressman from Wyoming – on the board of directors.[8] It, arguably, was a Casey-Cheney gambit with Van Andel as a front. The Jamestown Foundation recruited defectors to the CIA from among foreign secret-service officials and bureaucrats.

CIA ASSETS DEVOS AND VAN ANDEL RECRUIT TALENT AND VOTES TO WESTERN MICHIGAN

The names DeVos and Van Andel appear on dozens of building fronts, street signs, posters for events, and newspaper headlines in Grand Rapids – the closely linked families long ago began putting their stamp on the city. The stamp they evidently want is, *smart people who believe in money,* and the DeVoses and Van Andels make a point of recruiting such people to live in western Michigan. In Grand Rapids, new arrivals are running many start-up businesses that were "incubated" in the DeVos-funded Downtown Market. DeVoses are financially behind multiple community-development organizations that have ample budgets for recruiting of suitable out-of-towners.[9]

---

6   An appointment entry in the Gerald R. Ford Post-Presidential Office Files, 1977-2007, reads "5/1/79: Amway Corporation – Washington, DC." A plausible theory holds that Ford gained office because the CIA wanted him there – instead of Richard Nixon, who had finally withdrawn troops and, in the eyes of the fanatic cold warriors, contributed to the U.S. being defeated in Vietnam (where the CIA had gone all-out, killing 29,000 civilians in the Operation Phoenix headed by Ted Shackley). The theory holds that the Shackley wing of the CIA fed information to Bob Woodward's chief source, called Deep Throat, to bring down Nixon. But outside of that, the record suggests, Ford's being president protected a major CIA asset: the Amway company, owned by Jay Van Andel and Richard DeVos.

7   In 1983, however, DeVos and Van Andel pled guilty and paid $25 million in fines to Canada on a charge of tax fraud. Cf. *Vanity Fair,* September 26, 2018.

8   Wikipedia entry for William Geimer.

9   This is not just an aspiration. This agenda is a full-time job employing many people. Thirty-two full-time employees at 'Grand Rapids Kids' produce the West Michigan Relocation Guide for Families. Hello West Michigan's staff keeps a referral database for some 70 member companies. Says Spectrum Health human resources officer Pamela Ries,
        "Hello West Michigan is integral to our talent strategy."
The Right Place, which has Spectrum Health's CEO on its board, says,
        "Investing (in The Right Place) provides prominent positioning among the
        region's top corporations and access to key local leaders."
With many offices near Grand Rapids, Western Michigan's Lakeland Health conglomerate offers a

Even art is subsumed to the recruitment goal. In 2018, a $200,000 Art-Prize sponsored by an institute funded by the Dick and Betsy Devos Family Foundation drew 1,400 artists from 40 countries to Grand Rapids. Sam Cummings, business partner of Dick DeVos's brother Daniel, said,

> Our long-term goal is really to import capital – intellectual capital, and ultimately real capital. And (ArtPrize) is certainly an extraordinary tool.[10]

Perhaps the best is still to come. Likely the most powerful tool yet conceived for recruiting money-minded, educated folk to western Michigan will be the Grand Rapids Research Center (GGRC), set to open in 2021.

In February 2005, "stakeholders" in the planned GGRC included the afore-mentioned Michigan State University, the Van Andel Institute, and the DeVos-aligned organizations Spectrum Health and The Right Place, Inc.[11]

In what GGRC calls "the commercialization of science," it will arrange that as soon as a researcher makes a finding that can be "productized" – typically in a new electronic device – the researcher will be in line to get paid for it. By branding this revolutionary strategy to western Michigan, GGRC apparently hopes to create there a medical Silicon Valley, a new hub[12] of societal power and a continuous draw of like-minded migrants to colonize western Michigan. Figures supplied by The Right Place's Dave Riley show that this plan has already worked and should continue working.

In the Grand Rapids metro area, Riley said, to fill new jobs opening in research hospitals, 6,500 people arrived between 2014 and 2018, a remarkable population growth of 26 percent in that job category. The area's overall population grew by just 3.6 percent. In the DeVos-influenced "health care" or doctor's-office sector, 1,600 people arrived to work newly created jobs, an 8 percent growth in that sector. And in bio-tech research and development, a specialty of the Van Andel Institute, arrivals filled 200 new jobs, a 13 percent population jump in that sector.

All such new arrivals owe a debt for support of their economic future to the GGRC/Van Andel/DeVos power bloc. It is likely these thousands of new arrivals have voted and will vote the politics of their benefactors – Republican. Toward the political right, this has padded and will pad the

---

stout package of incentives to attract workers, including discounted General Motors automobiles.
10   This quote is taken from "The DeVos Family Reader," published by Grand Rapids Institute for Information Democracy.
11   MSU Web site
12   "What you're seeing is Grand Rapids being a hub for new innovations," said Jen Boezwinkle of Rockford Construction. Rockford Construction has built many DeVos/Van Andel projects in Grand Rapids.

electorate in western Michigan. Hillary Clinton lost to Trump in Michigan by only 10,700 votes in 2016. A shift to the right in this region is so recent that in 2016, in Grand Rapids's Kent County, Republicans said that, when Trump won the county's vote, they were "surprised." Whatever else the Trump crowd got up to, concerning electoral tampering, is still unclear.

On November 1, 2016, Trump's final campaign rally had come to Grand Rapids – at the DeVos Place Convention Center. Three years later, it was at the DeVos-sponsored Amway Center in Orlando, Florida, that Trump made his 2020 campaign kickoff.

Swing State – Florida

Like Michigan, Florida is an American security zone. This zone was established first in Miami around anti-Castro operations – including that odyssey in 1949 by Richard DeVos and Jay Van Andel – and in Orlando and Cape Canaveral around space rocketry and Walt Disney World. The establishment of such a security zone is evidenced by both an unusual contract won by George Wackenhut (on Wackenhut, see Introduction) and linked ventures by Disney company and the DeVos family.

In 1954 in Miami, George Wackenhut formed 'Special Agent Investigators', a detective agency. In 1960, CIA agent Paul Helliwell was transferred to Miami. Ted Shackley soon became Helliwell's boss in the CIA's JM/WAVE anti-Castro operations,[13] run out of Miami (this came long after Richard DeVos and Jay Van Andel had, as the record suggests, spied in Cuba, during their peculiar Caribbean yacht voyage of 1949). In 1963, Wackenhut Services, Inc. contracted to guard Cape Canaveral, home of U.S. space and Cold-War rocketry, some 48 miles from Orlando. In 1963, Walt Disney, who had long served as an FBI informant in Los Angeles,[14] also had his eye on central Florida.

After 1963, Wackenhut is believed to have worked on contract for the CIA, keeping dossiers on 2.5 million suspected American dissidents.[15] CIA agent Paul Helliwell, Ted Shackley's employee in JM/WAVE, also worked for Disney's company.[16] A certified lawyer, Helliwell, through fake companies, bought 40 square miles of central Florida for the planned Disney World and a huge buffer zone around it, then wrote charters for fake cities such that those 40 square miles owned by Disney were out of public jurisdiction –and

---

13   Spartacus Educational Web site.
14   *New York Times* May 6, 1993.
15   Free Government Information Web site, January 17, 2017.
16   Web site of "D23 – the Official Disney Fan Club"

outside the law.[17] In June 2005, Rob Jacobs, at the time chief of Florida's Bureau of Fair Rides Inspection, acknowledged of Disney World, "We don't have the authority to close the park down or close the rides."[18]

Federal law enforcement, too, deferred to Disney security, seeking out Disney's advice on "biometrics" and, after 9/11, using Disney biometrics to identify individuals through computer records of unique characteristics.[19]

DeVos and Florida

In 1991, like water welcoming a duck, the central-Florida security zone received Richard DeVos. DeVos came in big, buying a ball team – one with a Disney-referenced name, the Orlando Magic.[20] Soon, just as in Grand Rapids, Michigan, many *buildings* and institutions in Orlando displayed the *names* of DeVos or his Amway company.[21]

DeVos interests and Disney interests became increasingly combined – ostensibly beyond commercial interests.

The cover of a 1968 phonograph record of a Richard DeVos speech to the Junior Achievement Club (note the crown effect).

Planning EPCOT city next to Disney world, Walt Disney said his goal was to create more than a new amusement park – it was "creating a new America."[22] The America "sold" by the DeVoses resonates with the America envisioned by Walt Disney. Each of the two empires pushed the vision

---

17   TD Allman, in "Finding Florida," *Atlantic Monthly Press*, 2013.
18   Ibid.
19   *The Canadian Press*, September 5, 2006.
20   The reference is to Disney's "Magic Kingdom." This is an expression also favored by Christian evangelicals.
21   Sep 6, 2018 *Press Herald*, Orlando.
22   Ibid. to 5.

of a magical world, free from care. DeVos and Van Andel always touted Amway as a route to freedom from bosses – and after President Ford's probable influence in the Amway federal decision, combined with Disney's absolute power, this magical dream could extend to freedom from the law – always a basic tenet of Not-Exactly-the-CIA.

By 2010, the DeVos/Disney combine had talked county officials into funding Amway Center, a big new Orlando venue hosting pro sports and international conventions and featuring a huge, glossy entrance area called "Disney Atrium."

In September 2018, Richard DeVos died, but in Orlando his son Daniel was chairman of the basketball team Orlando Magic and, alongside Disney World, top contributor to a local Republican political action committee. Marking the tone of this central-Florida milieu was the U.S. Department of Homeland Security offering of 18 new jobs in Orlando as of June 27, 2019.[23]

Since 2010, Orlando has grown faster than all but a few American cities.[24] Just in 2016 and 2017, its metro-area population grew by more than half a million.[25]

How does all this stand to affect future presidential elections, in which it is highly likely Florida will continue to be a swing state?

Immigrants and future US elections

Among persons with backlogged green-card applications, more than 530,000 are from either China or India, and among US immigrants receiving green cards in 2017, China had 6 percent, Cuba 6 percent, and India 5 percent.[26]

In Florida, the record suggests immigration is adding conservative voters during the 2020 election cycle and will continue to do so.[27] The record suggests these conservative voters are being recruited, much the same as in Michigan. Recall that in western Michigan, recruitment comes via community-development organizations such as Hello West Michigan and The Right Place, largely DeVos-funded.

---

23   Indeed.com Web site.
24   Statista.com Web site.
25   Orlando Economic Development Commission. From 2016 to 2017, Orlando's four-county region – Lake, Orange, Osceola and Seminole – grew by 2.3 percent to more than 2.5 million people.
26   July 10, 2019 Migration Policy Institute.
27   Latino immigration tends to add liberal voters nationally, it is often noted, but in Florida, Cuban immigrants have voted Republican for many years. As the original refugees from Castro's victory age and die, however, the demographic is changing.

The EB-5 Visa

An easy road to voting rights is the EB-5 visa, lobbied for by real-estate developers and overseen by a division of Homeland Security. EB-5 is known as "cash for visa" and it is supported and exploited by the Trump family.

Many early users of EB-5 visas were millionaire Chinese.

Kushner Companies

Begun by President Trump's son-in-law Jared, Kushner Companies, along with China's Qiaowai Group and the Florida-based company U.S. Immigration Fund (USIF), is drawing Chinese millionaires to the EB-5 program.

Qiaowai bills a Kushner Companies development project in which it seeks EB-5 investors as "supported by the government, created by a star developer."[28] In Beijing in May 2017, Qiaowai, a defendant in a U.S. racketeering lawsuit involving EB-5 visas,[29] ejected U.S. reporters from a publicly advertised gathering of prospective EB-5 investors in the Kushner Companies project.[30]

As the *Washington Post* puts the matter,

> A lot of… lobbyists, consultants, and lawyers… get paid to entice wealthy foreigners into applying for the (EB-5) visas, and to persuade Congress to renew it each year.[31]

Around 10,000 EB-5 visas are available per year, allowing immigration for an applicant, a spouse, and all unmarried children under age 21.

In Florida, the Department of Homeland Security has approved around 80 agencies as "EB-5 Regional Centers".[32] Many an EB-5 Regional Center is simply a large development company that is government-approved to manage a pool of investors in a particular project of that company. Much development in Florida is funded by EB-5 visa investor pools.

In recent years, each of Florida's EB-5 Regional Centers has generated at or near its maximum of 40 EB-5 immigrant visas per year[33] (this totals

---

28   March 1, 2019 Bisnow South Florida Web site.

29   Kushner Companies is not a defendant in the suit, *Makhsous v. Mastroianni et al*, U.S. District Court for the Northern District of Illinois, No. 19-cv-01230.

30   CNBC, May 7, 2017.

31   *Washington Post* February 12, 2017.

32   EB-5 Investors Web site, January 11, 2019. The stated idea is that wealthy investors seeking to immigrate buy into a coming project that will create jobs (in theory, the immigrant gets a visa for helping create those jobs).

33   *Washington Post*, September 5, 2014.

3,000 or so EB-5 immigrants arriving in Florida per year during recent years, each eligible after 5 years for citizenship and voting).

The record suggests, then, that at least several thousand people who arrived in Florida on EB-5 visas between 2007 and 2011 matured into Florida voters between 2012 and 2016 – wealthy people, and thus disposed to vote for Trump. And, there's no reason to suppose such a pattern is not repeating – with more thousands of EB-5 Florida residents maturing into voters during the years 2016 and 2020.

Orlando and EB-5 Arrivals From India

In recent years, for many developers seeking EB-5 investment recruits for projects near Orlando, India has become the No. 1 target. Central-Florida developers have visited cities in India including Delhi, Mumbai, and Bangalore, to meet real estate agents with clients seeking to emigrate to the Orlando area by investing in EB-5 development projects. Orlando, with its Disney presence, is a hotbed of EB-5 visa use. The Orlando area is even home to ShantiNiketan, the nation's first gated retirement community developed specifically for Indian-American seniors. Indian-American votes in 2016 heavily favored Hillary Clinton, but since then Trump's aggressive talk on Pakistan has impressed Hindu Americans who see Islamic extremism as the biggest threat to the U.S. and to India.[34]

On August 21, 2016, a Web article referring to Indian-Americans was headlined, "There's One Group of Minority Immigrants in the U.S. that is surprisingly Pro-Trump."[35] Less than two months later, on October 15, 2016, Trump addressed a rally in New Jersey organized by the Republican Hindu Coalition.

A second special-visa type, the H1-B1, is in play here – Shalabh Kumar of the Republican Hindu Coalition is pushing Trump to shorten the path to citizenship for H1-B workers, and in January 2019, Trump promised he would assure citizenship for H1-B visa holders (a majority of whom are from India), saying,

> H1-B holders in the United States can rest assured that changes are soon coming which will bring both simplicity and certainty to your stay, including a potential path to citizenship.[36]

---

34   *Washington Post* October 14, 2016.
35   Quartz Web site
36   Posted on Twitter, January 11, 2018

In gratitude, Kumar has promised Trump $25 billion to help build a border wall, money to be raised by the Hindu-American community.[37]

A former Miss India poses with President Donald Trump and Shalabh Kumar of the Republican Hindu Coalition

DISNEY AND SPECIAL-VISA IMMIGRATION FROM INDIA

"EB5 Regional Centre on the doorstep of Disney!" shouts Florida developer British Homes Group.

In February 2014, an "International Recruitment Team" from Disney company, which is a DeVos-family ally in central Florida, began recruiting in the Indian cities of Delhi, Mumbai, and Bangalore. Barely six months later, in June 2015, Disney World took the bold step of laying off 250 long-time employees and replacing each of them with an Indian worker who held an H1-B visa.[38]

Disney lobbyists engineered the H1-B visa type and couple of other special visa types, the J visa and the Q visa. Disney lobbyists, in 1961 and again in 1990, teamed with the United States Information Agency – whose mission was combating communism through "cultural exchange" – to win new visa types (the J, the H1-B, and the Q) for cultural exchange earmarked especially for Disney World's hiring of "cultural ambassadors" for its Epcot World Showcase.[39] Participants in Disney's 2007 Cultural Representative Program held about 54 percent of the 2,412 Q visas that

---

37   *News 18* India, June 9, 2018
38   June 4, 2015, the *Economic Times* Web site and *New York Times*
39   Currently, about half of Disney's international "cast members" arrive on special Disney-engineered visas.
    Florida Law Review, February 8, 2013; "The Wonderful World of Disney Visas." Also cf. Immigration Daily Web site, "The ABCs of Immigration."

the United States granted during that year.[40] Through diligence, Disney hires, over time, can parlay such visas to citizenship and voting rights.

In 2018, Disney used the photo of a handsome young man, apparently of Indian origin, in founding "Disney Aspire."

The Disney Look

This photo from the "Disney Aspire" Web site on a page called "Disney Careers" officially represents "The Disney Look," according to the Web site. On the site, in one non-copyable version of this photo, the phrase "The Disney Look" is emblazoned in yellow in the lower left corner of the photo.

The "Disney Aspire" program helps new Disney workers gain fluency in English and in U.S. history with assistance from the University of Central Florida (which features a DeVos Sports Business Management degree program). The "Disney Aspire" education program apparently is designed to enable new Disney workers to eventually pass a citizenship exam and make a career at Disney if they so aspire. With President Trump at work on shortening the H1-B path to citizenship, the record suggests that recruitment under the H1-B and Q visa types, along with the EB-5, will pad Florida's Indian-immigrant voting rolls for future elections.

The record shows that, just as with the DeVos/Van Andel combine in western Michigan, actions of the Disney/DeVos combine in central Florida have served and will serve to import Republican votes to those states. It's unclear whether this result fairly can be said to stem from conscious intent (Richard DeVos tended to say "God" guided his actions) but DeVos's daughter-in-law Betsy, Trump's secretary of education, has stated flatly her desire and intention to influence elections, and Disney World hiring practice clearly evidences profiling in favor of Indian immigrants.

---

40   Ibid.

CUBA

Immigrants from Cuba to Florida used to vote nearly 100-percent Republican, but for Trump in 2016, that percentage was down to 54 percent.[41] Perhaps as a consequence of the fact that the Florida Cuban-immigrant community is liberalizing rapidly, President Trump effectively halted a family-reunification program slated to allow 20,000 Cuban immigrants per year to the U.S. Trump did this by withdrawing nearly all American Embassy officials from Cuba after, in May 2018, several of those officials complained of sudden, mysterious brain ailments.[42]

The same week the Castros overthrew Fulgencio Batista in Cuba on January 1, 1959, Amway was founded. In recent years, Amway has worked to turn Cubans into capitalists of its "multiple-level-marketing" variety, which narrowly escaped (with a little help from friends in high places) being ruled illegal in the US. In May 2014, Steve Van Andel, son of Amway co-founder Jay Van Andel, was a U.S. Chamber of Commerce delegate to Cuba to lay groundwork for American investment in the island.[43] And, in August 2018, some 168 Amway capitalists from southern Florida were part of another delegation to Cuba.[44]

Donald Trump's base believes he simply opposes immigration. But the record shows that Trump, the DeVos/Van Andel/Erik Prince combine, and others of that stripe – whose interests are continually served by Not-Exactly-the-CIA – quietly manipulate immigration to their perceived advantage, with significant consequences likely for future U.S. elections.

---

41   Pew Research Center Web site.
42   Some of these US officials were undercover CIA agents. Studies of the brains of those afflicted showed a pattern of trauma unique to medical science (New York Times, July 23, 2019). US Embassy officials in China suffered the same symptoms around the same time. If these officials were attacked by an enigmatic weapon, it is unlikely on its face that either Cuba or China is solely responsible – Cuban agents have no interest in harming U.S. officials in China, and vice versa. For an attack scenario, that seems to leave only a Cuban-Chinese concerted action – possible, but for various reasons unlikely – or action by NE-CIA – despite the fact that some CIA agents were injured; a slight sacrifice for a large concealment effect.
43   Granma Web site May 28, 2014.
44   El Lumpen Web site, July 2019.

Index